to be in this number

✦ also by alane rollings

to be in this number

alane rollings

TriQuarterly Books
Northwestern University Press
Evanston, Illinois

In gratitude, and for all their works of vision, homage to Saul Bellow, Janis Bellow, Reginald Gibbons, Cornelia Spelman, Jeanne Garlington, Henry Garlington, David Malament, Jody Stewart, Michèle Powell, Lisa Ruddick, Peter Stitt, Richard Strier, and Richard Stern

Northwestern University Press
Evanston, IL 60208-4170

Copyright © 2005 by Alane Rollings. Published 2005 by Northwestern University Press. All rights reserved.

Printed in the United States of America

10 9 8 7 6 5 4 3 2 1

ISBN 0-8101-5154-5 (cloth)
ISBN 0-8101-5155-3 (paper)

This book is an imaginative composition. Some real events are depicted, but no real persons, since the most complex fictional character is infinitely simpler than the simplest human being.

Library of Congress Cataloging-in-Publication Data

Rollings, Alane, 1950–
      To be in this number / Alane Rollings.
          p. cm.
      Includes bibliographical references.
      ISBN 0-8101-5154-5 (cloth : alk. paper) — ISBN 0-8101-5155-3 (pbk. : alk. paper)
          1. United States—History—20th century—Poetry. I. Title.
PS3568.O539T6 2005
811'.54—dc22

                                                                                        2005010004

♾ The paper used in this publication meets the minimum requirements of the American National Standard for Information Sciences—Permanence of Paper for Printed Library Materials, ANSI Z39.48-1992.

For my beloved husband, heart of my heart and soul
all the family
and my other sisters and brothers

contents
a chain

part **I**

I made a covenant with you . . . and you became mine.

—Ezekiel 16:8

I realize I don't even answer half your questions . . . I like Hopkins
(to answer one) particularly a sonnet beginning, "Margaret, are you grieving
Over Goldengrove unleaving? . . . [It is Margaret you mourn for"].

—Flannery O'Connor, a month before her death

I

sweetness night and day

I thought I inhabited my thoughts alone.
But those whose deaths I felt I'd die of,
since I hadn't said or done as much as love required,
live so vividly in me that others seem comparatively unreal.
Each death had left me over-swept with pain.
All my senses ceased receiving anything but pain.
Day, dust, night, love, time, thought: pain. Since I hadn't loved enough,
I had no right to suffer it, no choice but to suffer it.
I studied the lost faces, soft and hard and vague as faces.
Their gazes asked for nothing, but needed sweetness night and day.

My Dead, having lived, must be kept, somehow, alive.
As towns grow bright at sundown, drawing dwellers on dark outskirts
into their lit-up hearts, I pulled my Lost toward my center,
shared with them my blood, sweat, breath, and vulnerability.
Hoisting them around like a bag of newborn lambs
sticking noses out to nuzzle me, I asked them what I've asked
since I was born—*Why was I born?*
Except that I was carrying them, we were not that different.
I gave them constant reassurance of their actuality, while in my mind,
I redid everything I'd done and said.

They observed me with the rapt attention of the ignorant,
then flickered like a moving picture's strips of sun and shadow. They filled me
with their absences, then led me to a countryside where breezes left
the baby's breath untouched, yet brought, in unexpected gusts, solace
through the morning haze. No low-wheeling hawk ruffled up the goldenrod
or stopped a jacaranda from dropping violet petals upon a herd of yaks.

Afternoons, we'd mosey through the towns along the waterways—
replicas of those upon opposing shores—with pre-grief sorrow,
knowing that, at sundown, all the towns, absorbing our departures,
would glow with loneliness for us, matching ours for them.

The towns were evanescent: ghosts of roses on a trellis. Yet each
connected with a road that met another road running to another river,
every river bearing cradles, trucks, deer mice, gates, God knows what
atop its currents as it rushed through poplars, boxwood, bluegums,
taking shortcuts through the wide landscape—where life and death
took place—into a broader vista where imagination overtakes events.

The nights and days that gathered there
illuminated every passing moment.

But back within the genuine atmosphere where I'd been raised,
whole weeks were fading out and blaming me: I hadn't lived them.

I'd been holding out for more: an adequate good-bye
and sweetness day and night.

I'd call to my companions: *Courtney, Leanne, Arthur, Raman,
Lynda, Helen, Aunt Rowena, Uncle Wayne, Aunt Evelyn, Uncle Robert* . . .

I'd become a crowd; I was three generations
waking up in a different spot each hour
to the sky's unbroken solitude. Journeying together, we traversed
the glistening drifts of sand of our untrammeled sweep of land
whose headstrong rapids wouldn't let one kingfisher go under.
How could I let my Lost get lost once and for all?

I had more to do and say!

But Grandmother and the others I'd been born to bear—
though often in bad moods, they needed love anyway—

grew impatient with me: Needing love,
I'd used them to protect my isolation.
And all they'd been to me was not at all like who they'd been.

      As a last, magnanimous gesture, they circled me,
neighing inconsolably. Then, on wobbly, purebred legs haunch-high
in black-eyed Susans, they crisscrossed through a mist-wall
and stumbled off the landscape one by one.

      What they'd been was me. The only way to keep them
was to hold as closely as I could
all the borrowed elements that recompose me by the hour
on this substantial planet where I live.
      Gardens here saturate the twilight air with scents
of morning glories, tiger lilies, foxfire, larkspur, trillium—
      as if sundown could be overcome
or anyone could love enough
in such a little bit of time, and in the limits of this place
whose sweetness night and day,
when love moves through in infinite streams,
nothing can exceed.

2

fire in the water

For this is the country where the age of the internal combustion engine has come into its own, where every boy is Barney Oldfield and the girls wear organdy and batiste and eyelet embroidery and no panties on account of the climate . . .

—Robert Penn Warren, *All the King's Men*

Ten years before the Crash, after an eclipse made Relativity a certainty, the marks of Civil War had been erased in Mississippi.

Riverside, a father slept, depressed; a mother sold Dry Goods. As she sashayed to town and back, her swinging hips split the world: *Yes/No; Apple Betty/Lake of Hell;* pot pies for the poor/no cokes, no smokes, no radio for men—Rebels—always squelched.

Riverside, their boy picked up New Orleans' radio ragtime. Home, *she* waited, radiant, with his "birthright": Noah, Job, Abraham . . . rising by "begats" over wives and Kings to Chronicles and Acts, past Judges up the Prophets' pointers to Ezekiel's wheels—the big one, turning stars, and the others, interlocked with every worldly cog. The mechanism, overtaxed at every joint, sapped his soul.

He poled his raft toward riverboats. Pushed by steam, their engines turned the paddle wheels that cranked the siren songs out of calliopes. He sounded shoreward; cemetery-cities looming there scared him home.

Deep in downed pecans, she waited, night-gowned, in a backyard gang of ghosts: mothers nudging sons to sew the gashes that *their* fathers cut—*specter*-fathers still expecting these grown daughters to appease the spirits of *their* mothers—bullied speechless by *their* fathers, hounded by *their* mothers . . .

So each—living, men, women, dead—battered and was beaten by the shame and blame inevitable in 2-by-2 existence.

6

Off he ran. Riverside, branches danced on cumulus; a bobolink
was pining; a kingfisher, sapphire-winged, thrashed his bait-fish catch;
the boy freed a fox that wept, *Spring the trap; patch me!*

Gusts whipped up the rain they spewed. The 3-yard stream soon
overfilled into a 10-yard water wall, falling right and left, and then
abandoning both sides. Stranding boats on bucking sand, it flooded 40 levees.
It sucked barns up and dropped bulls down on 18-wheelers drowning on I-75.
Louisiana cried: *Evangeline!*—she lay bleeding. *Plaquemine!*—6 feet down.
New Orleans!—as lonely as a Lamentations town. *Her* living floated with
her dead, spread the dogwood-catfish South with bile. And all that
Spanish moss, in fact, hadn't yet absorbed the Mess of 60 years before.
The hurricane, tossing twisters, ran off to the Gulf. The boy raced
back to riverside, where waves rolled over fireballs—main streets,
pickup trucks, twin beds—then spat out wheelchairs, quilts, fig trees,
fractured girls, dismembered boys . . .

Mid-river, under frazzled power lines, business ledgers whirled.
They'd never logged a single heart's combustion!
But under private waters, he was crackling toward an inner blaze.
Moans and sea-songs, always waiting up for him, rammed his lungs
and disordered all of Numbers' numbers. Shamed and blamed by fantasies,
he picked up, by Model T, the road. The hungry, comeback beat of jazz
was throbbing on the radio. To and fro, he carted "balm-from-Gilead"—
water!—to the hard-hit, to tent cities. Doctoring *his* people—
everybody—let him snap back into socket.
In his head, on the phantom line between 2 tiny hammers
that had twanged to his Mamma's cry—*Baby!*—
he felt himself—his millstone—finally centered.

Near the end of a Depression it would take a war to finish,
he hauled his expectations to New Orleans. On Clio Street, beside a girl
as sweet as honeydew, he parked his ancient Packard. By radio,
Swing sang, *It's behind you:*

The Chasm—as personal as nerves etched by friction,
burned by want, burst by hurt, and added up by 1,000s on a life-wave
reeling down 10,000 years. The Chasm that divides the race in two
and multiplies suffering and passion by each other . . .

She shifted half an inch toward *yes*.
In self-defense, he alarmed her: *YOU CAN'T TOUCH MY DIAL!!*
   Might as well try picking up what arced above them,
linking all the cities: a big black bag of heaven's sea,
leaking fire through star-pricks.

3

page-a-minute

An emperor besieged a town. He told the women they could
leave, carrying what they could. They came out of their houses
with their husbands and children on their backs.

—old tale

I came out of my mother on my own.
I used to think I'd lived my past alone.

When she met Daddy—'41—between Euterpe Street and Terpsichore,
her green eyes tilted upward. Soon, they had two small girls, then four ('54).
At the birth of Pamela and Janet, her 1st twins, her navel, a line, grew circular.
      They'd skid, north–south, along our Georgia hall. She'd pace,
east–west, the kitchen, praising all their steps. Catch them in a lockhold?
She'd lock one up, one down, toss one *The Brothers Grimm,* the other
Mother Goose, chiming to both 5-year-olds: *Maybe you'll escape!*

      Soon, by Ford, we all made Daddy's house calls to the "coloreds,"
the hard-hit. Pinpoint's red clay roads—overgrown with green gardenias—
turned to Isle o' Hope's shell-paved alleys, their deeper green magnolias.
"Shalimar" from Mamma's hair, unbobbed by speed, increased the sweetness
as it flew (as I—9—knew). That fall, Ol' Lady cut the romance short:
      Well, sit all day in the Mercury, if it makes you King of the Castle!
Half an hour, I sat singing: *I'm the king and she's the big, mean Communist!*

      Soon, spying through the nursery door hinge, I—11—watched her
kidnap Robert. She bounced, kissed, hoisted him, then cha-cha'd with him
up and down our row of antique desks. Then it hit me: dancing shoes

could dance you—*me*—west o' the sun and 6 feet under . . .

Soon, her Singer spun a costume for *his* spinning twin: Ellen, in a tutu,
draped in crimson tulle, became the Firebird, grand-jêtéing into riddles' eyes:
What turns common things to what you want? Then what you'll lose?

What marched off the Silver Screen to Gaston Street to Victory Drive
to Habersham to White Bluff Road and into *me*, collapsing with my Moon Pie
at the Minit Store? What *Time* was it, Old Witch? '63! I'd bled, fainted, tasted
iron—and I thought Time was *mine!* A minute in the cooler, and I staggered
home, to the attic—*Leave me be! I'm on a streak!*—bounding down to rev the
Deuce Coupe through the fence to Largo Drive to Abercorn toward Beaufort.
  Dear Diary, Today Mamma's wicked witch-hand whacked me.

✦ ✦ ✦ ✦ ✦

(My Post-it Note—'85) *All I ever did for you was to scream bloody murder.*
Some Red Rover sent her over—over all her griefs into my ocean-deep emotions.
  Came a spring ('97), we six kids caught her call for all of us, ran home.
Loved the same, we wore our different versions of her face, loved the same.
  Mamma—old; too sick too soon, in Daddy's nightshirt, prison-striped,
and her pale-as-duck-down hair—took a baby step toward us—back into
the March of Time—then sank into the arms of the violet girls in bonnets
        that *her* mother—
her Melpomene—had whipstitched on *her* daughter's quilt. *Mamma's* first,

her fair Cynthia, held her as she fell. Now, in the guest room, she's asleep.
Her closed eyes flutter: left/right, black/white, bright/pale, page on page . . .
  Beneath a scrapbook photo, clipped ('42) from the *Times-Picayune:*
*The treasure of Polymnia Street: Page-a-Minute Irma Lee, her midnight mane
crowned in Pink Sensations by the former Secretary Queen of storied New Orleans.*
  Mamma's secret reading stops—she's awake—and starts: she's back
with images that haunt, fade, return, return, return, return, return, and then,

dropping the iron lace of inconsolable, planet-core emotions—stop again.

Full stop.

Who killed Cock Robin? Who pilfered silver apples from the moon,
then flung us out into blank space to fetch them?
    Golden Ogre, leaping greedily through stars—*her* stars—a lantern group,
suspended there at my 1st-story window—*her* view—just east o' the
North Wind's cookie—*her* moon—it's *You!* And here, in my high school spiral
binder—page by 8-by-11-inch moonlit page—I see impressions of your teeth . . .
    And everywhere, with *all* my sensible, common-sensical diamonds—
my moon, stars, *mother*—I'm caught inside Time's crooked bite.

    January; '67; Henry Street; Savannah. Long red light. She wore
turquoise (store-bought; Tall Girls' Shop) and waltzed around her kids as we
got taller. A bus rushed out of who knows what, jumped the curb, drenched
her face, and swirled her swept-up skirt—unveiling Mamma's skinny legs,

our helplessness.

4

gang of four

White coral bells upon a slender stalk,
Lilies of the valley deck my garden walk.
Oh, don't you wish that you could hear them ring?
That will happen only when the faeries sing.

—from "White Coral Bells," an old round

By accidents—our births—I found them not long afterward.
They had my blood. To warm it, I pressed my chest to theirs.
To read my thoughts, you'd have thought these four the only kids.
Big Sis, I'd fetch my gang for visitors and start a round:
White coral bells . . . I sang. Then their *White coral bells* . . .
rang out, chiming to my *lilies of the valley* . . .

Among the yard's blue gums, the twins scattered and regrouped.
One Monday, when they left the house, a cloud bank rushed off
to the woods, fast-forward, hauling off the sky. Someone must have vanished!
I cried and gasped for half an hour. My gang had gone to school.
One September, I left *them,* high-stepping at the tetherball.
From college, I was still transfixed each time their faces crossed
my thoughts. Then when, in flickering mixer strobes, classmates hit
familiar notes, their new features also gripped my consciousness. Our talk—
with intermittent strains of melodrama, comedy, bravado, revelation—
rose above the thumping Rock to drop me, fast-reverse, on my inside
backstretch, a private, mental space, never mine alone for long.

That sprawling lawn, always tended, always overgrown,
still opens wide to strangers who can ferry, by any small resemblance,
my brother or a sister up from memory. Then two eternal six-year-olds

and two eternal eight-year-olds step forth from recessed orchestras
of hollyhocks and 4 o'clocks and into my awareness, a resounding, central pit.

   Passersby who bring to mind my sisters and my brother
are tied to me by this: *each is bound to others.* Link by link, not thinking—
flash—I make them "gang of friends."

   In imagined rows of time-lapse photos, they unfold.
Then they begin enfolding me, overcoming my resistance to a tie that might
become too taut—if not too slack—to last for long.

   For that moment—a chord prolonged by echoes—everyone
is *one of us.* All of us, by one spell, are held: kin, friends, enemies, and some,
the peace of whose strong lives had promised peace, in time, for me . . .

   Suddenly, their time had gone:
Linton and Leona, Imre and Maria, Alberto, Edward, Kate, Peter, John, Omelia—
"mine" long enough to call them "mine"—all had vanished.

   Then there they were once more! In the sister/brother aura,
everyone was backlit by my sudden recognition on a wide, brief terrace,
ever-green with fragile bonds that strengthen in their blossoming.
Momentarily, in the lengthening sweep of consciousness, all of us rock all of us
in full refrains of baby's breath, counter-pointing lilies of the valley . . .

   Stepping out in my interior, I become a crowd—
sistered, brothered by all kinds in a long-as-life exchange
whose resonance intensifies a sympathy that heightens resonance.

   Among the everlastings scattered now though city grass,
the sun has thrown the shadow of each blade.

   Hiding low, ladybugs and lacewings trill and still.

   Crystalline soprano tones they suspend upon the calm
represent Ephemera
entering the realm of the Perpetual.

   It's a self-accompaniment that charms their tiny, waking lives
into split-second dreams, recurring endlessly . . .

(I'd suggest, *Let's rest and make a chain . . .*)

And I know how,

(We'll braid the stems . . .)

with four who take me back to when I didn't have to learn to love alone

(How long?)

I got so much, it's taking years to spend it.

crossover

I

Pinpoint was stuck inside Savannah.

Celia, who was colored—in her gray maid's uniform—
and whom I loved, cell by cell, and hugged and clutched each day
before she caught the bus at 4 o'clock—was stuck in Pinpoint.

Forty-eight United States were waving at me: *Come on over!*
White, I might go anywhere, be anyone.

Just by getting knocked up, or a job at the Auto Show, or murdered,
I could be a symbol for all girls.

At Celia's Church Revivals, '55–'58, someone always got the spirit—
shrieked his soul in tongues. We all joined in: our mouths went dry and up
from down-deep rose our pleas to God—*School! Gold Tooth! Blue Cadillac!*

Linking arms, we marched through Pinpoint, belting out together
"When the Saints Come Marching In." *(Oh, I long—to be—in that number . . .)*

In sixth grade, I sneak-listened every day to my transistor:
Little Richard and Chuck Berry, raised on Muddy Waters
and his amplified guitar, were high-hurdling music's bars.
I started dancing big.

King Elvis went to Germany; Buddy Holly's plane went down,
taking Ritchie Valens. Temping in Atlanta, I'd move up as surely
as I'd ascend to heaven. Patsy Cline's plane went down.

Emigrants pushed into towns, knocking over fences;
my landlord's high-rent low-rise rose from tenements he'd razed.

Urban gaucho, he fulfilled, with phrases from the Hit Parade,
my romantic fantasies. I was soon his willing calf,
love-lassoed on his saddle.
When he dropped me in his dust, I got to watch him gallop off.

Otis Redding's plane went down. Celia's husband's other wife
hightailed it out of Pinpoint with their money.

Little Stevie Wonder made the Top Ten at eleven.
Crossover was hot. The '60s twisted, shouted.
Rick Nelson's plane went down; Bruce the Boss revved us all: *Go!*
From every closet, reservation, slum, and Chinatown in fifty states,
we headed for head-on collisions. Soon, in pile-ups nationwide, white-boy
emperors crashed against gay architects, judges, and no-benefit princesses;
sports champs crashed with Lesbian divas, comics, native Americans . . .
From the bottom, Resurrection City's saints tried to lead us in a round:
Do Lord, O, do Lord, O do remember me . . . But some of us, near the top,
would not intone with others, chanting from the fringes, *I got a home
in Gloryland that outshines the sun, O Lordy* (but no wreck to sing in).

Jim Croce's plane went down.
My old evictor crashed on me. I was still his kind of girl—
deferential, vulnerable, a paycheck from the pavement. He offered me
a sixth-floor walk-up with a glimpse of crosstown ocean:
stop and go and blooming yellow, red, green, yellow, red
across the Mississippi and beyond the Blue Ridge Mountains . . .

Harry Chapin's; Lynyrd Skynyrd's; John Denver's planes went down;
they joined Mayfield, Gaye, and Cooke and formed a band in heaven.

Tina Turner rose up solo; Prince reclaimed his crown;
Michael Jackson lost some black. They all, from the tops of charts, rattled
basement bars to Aretha Franklin's beat *(r-e-s-p-e—)* into another century.

When Gospel Rock first made the News, it gave our tails a shake,
whether we were country, swing, soul, R&B—however alien we seemed.
America took in the Beatles, we took in the Rolling Stones.
Swapping blood, Pop's citizens high-stepped it up and up . . .

Some of us topped the charts. Some had not–Top Forty hearts.
Some of us, marching tall, came down wrong on brittle bones.
Acting out on Mother, Father, Celia—Us and Them—we packed
our fractures on their goat-frail backs. Why should we be stuck alone?

Some of us got strong enough to trip our weaker friends—
so we could clutch, alone, Jacob's ladder (higher, higher).
Some of us hounded God: *Cross over!* So, one more time,
He left his Heaven-hood to join our crowded, lonely number.

So now we've got Him hog-tied on a rotten dock, God help Him.
He rocks above the drink!
A Pinpoint bum, he's lurching toward—*O, Lordy!!*—
His graveyard spiral down, down, down. He's calling:

Queen of Soul, sing us all some Golden Oldies!

6

blood sport

. . . my mind, striving for hours on end to break away
from its moorings, to stretch upwards . . .

—Marcel Proust

He heard his own whisper, rising from down deep: *Hit it!*—

and began, with a smash, his lifelong match. Next, a volley,
and the crowd outscreeched the egrets, crashing through an ironwood grove
beyond the California court.

He hit and hit, then hit it out: *Brilliant stroke, Idiot!*
With one more self-rebuke—*Lard ass, get off my back!*—he stepped into
the undergrowth, forgetting all his victories to obsess upon his sissy shots.
   The lady in the Padres cap, who watched his food through boyhood
and coached him for whatever game he grew up to be game for,
found him in a Cougar dugout playing One-Eyed Jack.

At 14, he'd played Sudden Death with Minnesota backboards.
The kid—like a white-tailed deer in 18-wheeler headlights—asked for it
from tennis bums: "Smack me!"
   Skidding, smacked, into the rough, he'd practiced, from a sand trap,
not wafting loopers to the loons submerged beneath the frozen lake.

Back on tour, he dashed for drop shots, jitterbugging,
touchdown style, when he upset the Favorites.
   On the circuit in New York, Vermont, the Carolinas,

18

he tangoed with his racquet down the alleys. He outsprinted chaos, then
mixed Serena-grace with Venus-grit to lope through Texas, pausing
in the central stretch to Jordan-dunk his quandary: *What's the point?*
    If he could fake out fatalism, he might win his Lady . . .

    But could he hold her face—his Luck—snow leopard–radiant
in that crowd of doubters? Back and forth, he danced for *Them;* she followed
with her gaze. They'd liked his heart when they first caught it, then began
to call—with no reversals—every call on every ball
that nipped, missed, or whacked the ground-sky net.

    Ohio: down in Sudden Death, he was begging his last lob,
Go back! Be a bullet; outrace my speeding errors! But he pounced again—
a Pennsylvania panther—to gently lay his fluff ball in the chalk dust.
    Why the fuss! Is it the Competitors—another Them—*who drive me
on and up and nuts? Or is it just the judgments of the court?*

    He'd die to follow *Ruth, Louis, Gehrig, Aaron, Joltin' Joe, Robinson,
Ali, Williams, Wilt the Stilt, Nadia, Magic, Rose, FloJo, the Hurricane*—another
Them—in perpetual motion past addictions to comparison that pushed them
past comparison and up the training hill of Walter Payton, then past blackjack,
past roulette, past enchantment, sports fans, fitness, game plans,
competition, progress, to a stratosphere where aspiration unwinds Time
and finally contends with Nothingness.

    Endangered gulls have chosen Carolina palms for fortresses.
    Shaded there with his life-mate, our world-class Ace, awaiting
his next match, is the ringside witness of some underdogs in fights-for-life:
    Echinodermata v. Waves
    The News: **HOLY MOTHER WINS AGAIN: A KNOCKOUT!**
    Tiny Starfish Showed Star Stuff, But Ocean Goaded Ocean: Go!
    (No One Could Outshout It)

Nearby, tagged for doom, a little swift nests in mid-trajectory.

Soon, our Champion Man begins brooding through the tournament—

I can't outwit consciousness, can't peek at Being's hidden hand, can't appeal
one thought to the Mother of all Law, can't not miss, can't hit for long, can't be They,
can't not be . . . **ONE MORE SUDDEN DEATH!** But just by thinking,

he pulls out a pair of Kings: *Tap it in like Arthur Ashe; take a Sammy Sosa bow,*

shadow-box through no-man's-land, waltz past all your rivals, then,
Arcing over Giant Pines Like Sentries Guarding Baseline—
Marble, Gibson, Babe, Budge, Butkus, Laver, Rosewall, Hogan, King, Borg, Gretsky,
Navratilova, Evert, Graff, Shoemaker, Mac, Tiger, Shaq, Capriati, Sampras, Agassi—
meet the spinner in suspense overhead and

HIT IT!

7

saint venus

> *Venus revolves around the Sun just as do all*
> *the other planets.*
>
> —Galileo Galilei

Conceived by history and the moon, the tiny female infant
was nicknamed "Drop of Mud"—to palliate disparagers.

Banned from hunts for centuries, she cleaned the kill. She didn't
play forbidden games—Old Maid, solo croquet—only the harmonium.
No school star, the little girl began to read her chart: *Dip into a pool of You,*
and you'll feed a multitude. Later, she awakened in a puddle of her blood.

Bleeding was like weeping. *Shut off in the shade of shame,* she couldn't
say *Ocean*—hexed, it could flood. Or let her wellspring drip into the river—
rotting crops. Tasting iron, she cursed her cramps. Not allowed to watch
a dump-dog gnaw her underpants, she scrubbed her ugliness into the floor.

Her flowers flowed from adolescent flesh, overdressed for any man
who'd stand up to the prophecy: *Glimpse a menstruant and unleash Chaos.*

No woods confused by woods, no Beyond that craved its blue,
could erase her self-disgust. Her lack became a wish—its object absent.
She'd tilt her unfixed form—as to a nova in the void—toward the Other.

Waltzing in a corset to the 20th Century, she became a Debutante:
one identity allowed her gender. Men caressed her petal-skin petal-thin
and left her wanting other hands upon her shame of wanting.

She was chosen; she became specific. As Princess Bride, the object
of a mass Desire, she was worshipped. Then, womanlike, she was stripped.
Clutching at her husband, she learned another shame: unshared oblivion.

She retched; swelled; hemorrhaged his heirs; recarved her figure.

Sickened by the *Globe* and *Mirror*'s killer archetypes—hard to prove,
harder to deny *(Witch! Seductress! Raving slut!)*—she heard voices: *Mother!*—

then met the meek, the maimed-by-mines—*We get hungry; we can't see.*
And the poor-in-spirit, rising up from Monster-arms that pinned them down
to hospice cots. And the ragtag kids-of-God, rocking on her angel-knee—
This is the way the hunters go: *Galloping! Galloping! Galloping!*

This is the way her lover proved her lunacy: he sold the News
her raptures—wiretapped—over him. All charity, the crowd cried *More!*

The palace split. Not from war: from lack. Not of bricks: of Being.
With everybody leeched by need, who'd stop the need, the bleeding?

Glorified, then storified by public adoration, the Princess got divorced—
then strengthened, blushed, glossed, enchanted, ranted, and dressed down
and up to bless the ravenous. Without a vision, perfect beauty, or infallibility,
Womanness—her version—was nurturing unconscious, common Want.

For eating universal wounds, she earned contingent gratitude.

A sweat-ring formed around her head. Saint Venus knelt to God.
His Fatherness, embracing her, merged with Longing, turned to Love . . .

The paparazzi, pining for control, were on her tail: *She's running!*—
Stop! Were the hunters—*Sister us!*—dumb enough—*Mother us!*—to imagine—
Lover us!—she could feed—*Deliver Me!*—a Soul, growling, howling in its pit?

She's out of breath! Trapped. *Our sovereign power—give it back!*
Spinning out, her Mercedes ricocheted, post to wall, flung her,
unstrapped, into steel that squeezed her breasts, spilt her chest, clamped her,
untransfigured, down. Untransformed into a laurel snatching at the sun—

vanished from an absent heaven—she wept into the vacant space in Space:
Don't let me weep alone!

Get a close-up of her blood!

8

the secret blackness of red roses

Woe that I have failed to kneel before you, inconsolable
Sisters, failed to more freely surrender myself in your
loosened hair.

— Rainer Maria Rilke, "Tenth Elegy" (early version)

I ran from Mamma, following my sister to the sidewalk.
Cynthia walked on to school; I went back to the den, to my chair
beside the bookcase with two doors, one wide open, hiding me.
There I read, as Cynthia had taught me, *Who Are You? (I am Downy Duck.)*

My mother [Eudora's] *sank as a hedonist into novels. She read Dickens*
in the spirit in which she would have eloped with him . . . St. Elmo
[popular Southern novel] *was not in our house. My mother was able*
to forgo it. But she remembered the classic advice given to rose growers on how
to water their bushes long enough: "Take a chair and St. Elmo . . . "

Mamma taught us kids "Boogie Woogie": one piano, separate duets.
"Frankie and Johnny were sweethearts." Pause—my left hand on her right wrist.

In the garden [Virginia's], *birds that had sung erratically and spasmodically*
in the dawn, now sang together in chorus, as if conscious of companionship, now alone . . .
Fear was in their song, and apprehension of pain, and joy to be snatched this instant.
They swerved high over the elm tree, singing together. Escaping, pursuing, pecking
each other, they turned high in the air, then dropped down and sat silent on the wall,
their bright eyes glancing, and their heads turned this way, that way . . .

We siblings smoked, ate paper, drank mouthwash, swapped blood,
chewed crumbs, called pebbles "pearls," and hid from Daddy when he was
a typical, heartbroken, driven, driving, and heartbreaking screaming King.

In my room, I left Ed Sullivan my laughing fits [*Last Will*]. He'd ushered
Madame Butterfly into our den. Daddy, Mamma, kids howled along joyfully.

24

When a fishbone stuck in her throat, making her cough so violently her face
turned scarlet and her eyes filled with tears, my father [Colette's] *brought his fist*
down on the table, shivering his plate to fragments and bellowing: "Stop it, I say!"

My mother, stopping choking, eating, breathing, always said, *I'm sorry!*
DADDY: *SHUT UP, IRMA LEE! stupid broad.* Lips pressed, she begged me,
Do not speak! Mutely, I recited my one Bible verse: *Jesus wept Jesus wept . . .*
DADDY: *JUST SHUT UP AND LEAVE!*

In my room, I renamed my mother "Herbal Tea." In the kitchen,
I questioned her repeatedly: *Herbal Tea, that ring in your nose—why wear it?*
SHE: *Do you mean the gold band in my Renoir snub that you've chosen to inherit?*
And Sister, look at the lips you could have had!
I: *The better to eat the leftovers—like* you, *Greasy Spoon?* [I'd rechanged her name]
SHE: *The better to do what* you'll have *to do—if you haven't finished you!*
I: *Have you finished my dress, Herbal Tea? Where is it?*

Who knew, at 10, what Simone W. knew: *that sympathy of the weak*
for the strong is natural, for the weak, in putting himself into the place of the other,
acquires imaginary strength. The sympathy of the strong for the weak, being in the
opposite direction, is against nature. Still, I could see in Greasy Spoon, a girl
of 20 waiting to have me—waiting still, 40, for me to stop laughing till they
dragged me from assembly. To stop mooing cowlike to the church choir.

So she talked her hick talk—*cryin' out loud!*—with my teachers!
I was waiting in my hula skirt, laughing fit to die—in *my* shame at *hers.*

Back in our backyard, she'd wait to meet halfway.
As she spoke, her face, alight with faith and an all-embracing curiosity,
was hidden by another, older face, resigned and gentle. "I can't remember whether
it was a family of crocus bulbs I planted there, or the chrysalis of an emperor moth.
Are you [Colette] *taking in what I say? You won't touch it?"*

"No, Mother."

She knew that I should not be able to resist, any more than she could, the desire
to know, and that like herself I should ferret in the earth of that flowerpot until it had
given up its secret. I never thought of our resemblance, but she knew I was

her own daughter and that I was already seeking that sense of shock, the quickened
heartbeat, and the sudden stoppage of breath . . . To lay bare and bring to light . . .

I sought another character, changed my name incessantly, couldn't find
my family in books. But Mamma, open-armed, glissaded, Jackie Gleason–style,
into the den, belting out, *Baby Baby! Daddy Daddy!*—pulling us, in '65, to supper,
past the TV, past each other, past Daddy's smiles, laughter, and applause for
all of "Mamma's Babies," to the dining room, no travelin' music. *And away we go!*

DADDY: *SERVE ME MILDEW, WOMAN, & SCRAPE IT OFF THE WALL!*

"Ruby" (a new me) went to her room, wouldn't show her face—my face.

IRMA LEE: *You say you're ugly, for cryin' out loud? How, with* you *inside you?*

Booming down the hall: *WHO STOLE MY SPOON? dumb female*

Like Emily, I didn't see *the Wound/* [Who was I?] *Until it grew so wide/*
That all of Life entered it [Idiot Bitch]—*and there were Troughs beside—*

20. Panic attack. Up the stairs I gasped to the black hole in the mirror.
Mamma, passing, stroked my shoulder: *Soft, soft shoulder! Love as hard as you can!*

I loved so—life so—CRYIN' OUT LOUD!

Wave crashes. [Virginia] *I wish I were dead! . . . This goes on; several times,*
with varieties of horror . . . The wave again! The irrational pain; the sense of failure as,
for example, my taste in green paint . . .

At last I say, watching as dispassionately as I can, take a pull of yourself.
No more of this . . . I brace myself to shove, to batter down. I march blindly forward . . .
it is not oneself but something in the universe that one is left with. It is this
that is frightening and exciting in the midst of my profound gloom, depression,
whatever it is . . . All I mean is to make note of a curious state of mind . . .

Twenty years, I noted the *Cleaving in My Mind—As if My Brain* (like
Emily's) *had Split./I tried to match it Seam by Seam—/But could not make them fit.*
Yet in ten, I recomposed our dismantled den; gramophone; TV; my wise Cynthia,
my Diary; I re-met Poe, the Brownings, sisters, brother, visionary
doctor-fathers, and my mother, singing backup to the vacuum cleaner:
Shall we gather at the ri—ver, the beautiful, the beautiful ri—ver?

The voices spelled "W-A-T-E-R" to my blind-dumb language-thirst.
With Simone, I read *The Book of the Dead: I've never spoken in a haughty tone.*

I've never been deaf to words of justice and truth. They spelled out *Beauty*
to all of those who labor, facing scorn, to be the roses whose rose-reds
grow deeper from the blackness they've absorbed.

Suddenly, dragging me, laughing, out of *La Bohème:* a man who sang
my name; poured hot chocolate; rocked me at the window, kissing, laughing—
Give me your croissant? (the beautiful, the beautiful); stood by me in the mirror
while I combed his hair; studied with me, line by line (the beautiful,
the beautiful) *The Critique of Judgment.* When we parted for a month,
he hailed my cab. I was wailing, fit to die: *That's my life waving there!*

My only faith [Simone W.] *had been to love the universe, beloved fatherland
of every soul. The result was that the irreducible quantity of hatred and repulsion
which goes with suffering and affliction recoiled entirely upon myself . . .*
      *This is so much the case that I absolutely cannot imagine the possibility
that any human being could feel friendship for me. I am all the more tenderly grateful
to those who accomplish this impossibility . . .*
      My Irma Lee. Old, sick, less forgetful, she gave up her gems—
The Smitten Rock that gushes! Bracelets opened; rings slipped off, and chains—
The trampled Steel that springs! She gave up her stories—ours—her statuettes:
frail saints; fragile birds. She played Ray Charles for Daddy.
SHE: *Don't give up on me!* DADDY: *Don't give up on* me*!* RAY: *Now I'm losing you.*
      [Simone de B.] *She knew what she ought to have said to God—"Heal me—
But thy will be done: I acquiesce in death." My* mother didn't acquiesce, *did not choose
to utter insincere words, but did not grant herself the right to rebel. She remained silent—*
then gave up the weight of the rose on the stem, the weight of the rain on the
rose that became my thought of her voice that held the world then spilled it—

      [Audre] *I have often wondered why the farthest-out position feels so right;
why extremes, although difficult and painful to maintain, are more comfortable
for me . . . What I really understand is a particular kind of determination.
It is stubborn, it is painful, it is infuriating, but it often works.*

My mother was a very powerful woman. This was so in a time
when that word-combination "woman" and "powerful" was almost inexpressible
in the white American common tongue . . .

As Mamma's flesh slid beyond my reach, she pushed me out,
promising, *I'm inside if you need me.*

> [Emily] *I meant to find her when I came—*
> *Death—had the same design—*
> *But the Success—was His—it seems—*
> *And the surrender—mine—*

And yet her dust—*all* my mothers' dust—casts a spell upon
the ache I still breathe in, with every breath, for her—for them—for me—
an ache that might have stopped my speech.

> [Emily] *To wander—now—is my Repose—*
> *To rest—To rest would be*
> *A privilege of Hurricane—*
> *To memory—and me.*

I've left the bookcase for the night. Up the stairs, Mamma's waiting.
Diva in her throat, she floats a lullaby of my descent through blood.
She pauses, takes a breath—*"Are you asleep?"*
"Yes, Mamma"—
for us to bind, with doubled thread, the beautiful, the Sublime.

part **II**

*It was only a violin, but I was sure that it was playing Bach. An andante,
I think, a halting tune in which the violin shadows itself . . . Whenever I heard
this andante I saw . . . a vertical line, fluctuating in width, then two lines dancing
close together, a line splitting apart and fusing . . . At certain moments both lines
become stronger and more plaintive, straining to get as far apart as possible.
Any moment this music will make another player out of thin air . . . But in the end
the illusion is not sustained, there is only one voice after all, and the violinist is alone.*

—Isabel Cole, on Bach's Sonata no. 2 in A Minor
for Unaccompanied Violin, played by Jascha Heifetz

*Least Village has its Blacksmith
Whose anvil's even ring
Stands symbol for the finer Forge
That soundless tugs—within—
Refining those impatient Ores
With Hammer and with Blaze—*

—Emily Dickinson

I was to get my answers to life and things in storms.

—Zora Neale Hurston

9

high romance and everlastingness

I'd burst in, hardly conscious of him hardly consciously removing,
from the desk, his feet, and from his mouth—to meet my kiss—a strong cigar.
What a month of May we'd made inside that August day!

　　Knowing where I stood—between the radio and microwave—
I mamboed, mop in arms. Any metamorphosis was possible.
Didn't marriage fuse romance to everlastingness?
　　While winter breezes nabbed the leaves
from peony trees outside the pantry window,
I tango-spun toward spring.

　　Let him dash for buses that dashed off with him. As governor of the den,
I suspected life in love was self-sufficient like no other—if there *was* another.
I *knew* there was no other so magnanimous. A little summer sun, dovetailing
through Venetian blinds, could stripe with light the kitchen table,
letting me dissolve into the Yangtze Gorges I was drawing
on a small tomato box from the grocery store.

　　If he vanished in a book, sorted pencils, sat in shorts before the fan,
or cursed the Bears all fall from his La-Z-Boy: betrayal. He was alien.
Staggering home from tennis in the spring, he'd meet his match: I'd be belting

out "Volare" from the bath I'd run for him. If I saw him at his desk, scribbling
in his tiny script, I had to tap-dance in. He'd kick me out—but only when
I'd listened to his *Tristan,* accompanied by compact disc.

Once again, winter. Face to corner, hands on ears, eyelids clenched,
I hibernated, like my mother, never wondering if he wondered where I was,
while I, asleep, grew conscious I had borne a snuggling cub.

Back by spring to Lincoln Center reveries, I wore white wings. I knew
I'd never bowed for any other crowd but him, applauding in my dreams.
When he slipped beneath my skin, I burst to bleed for him alone;
I'd sacrifice my inner life only on our double altar of attentiveness.
That fall, as I edited my stand-up comic daydream, I spilled his tea
upon him, mistaking for a china cup the hand I counted on to hold my own.

Cruising into our Aegean summer honeymoon, we'd landed on a
booked-up beach. We hardly slept—frightened, dressed—on someone's roof,
awakening transfigured by *our* island's glimmer-green on glistening blue.

Every time I pull my nightshirt overhead, he strums a tone poem
on my upraised arms. We jump onto the comforter as if into a skiff. He says,
Love-slave, we're free all winter. I say, *Let's clean house.* But, as one, we know
that we know, as one, our long hall's photos: Tanzania; Zambia; the Congo . . .
In comparison, the Japanese weeping cherry tree—my study view,
blooming fuchsia in the spring—has come to seem improbable.

Spying on him from between door hinges, I contemplate unlikelihood:
What's to stop his intellect from merging with my flightiness? His dignity and
my delight? Our substances /our spirits? Our separate, inseparable myths?
In winter, like my mother, I stuff door cracks with towels, don't go out
except to scrounge for facts to heat the Evening News. On that repast,
he's off to life's long fantasy before returning home, escapee from a storm.

Mamma's gone, and we've grown older, feeling no less young.

From spring to spring, my sweaters offer dresser drawers
their violets. His magazines have toured the house:

our villa, tilted on a rock. Our painting propped upon an easel,
stripped of all our other pictures superimposed and underneath, unveiling
a transparency that limits the reality it translates into masterpiece.

Constructed out of resonance fortified by sympathy heightened by
the resonance, this life resembles Life: an edifice with window screens
shimmying in heat that hums when dragonflies come by to drop
some dragonfly-wing dust.

10

world-class race

On an ancient notion, cookie-cut, "The Individual,"
Mother England nurtured Us—disappointed; ideal-struck: Romantics.
On our Redcoats, stained by Revolution,
Evolution threw new mud. Who *was* this Man-Ape, standing up,
naked in our faces, and calling, *I!* like *Us?*
We clutched our dogs—Toby, Ben-Hur, Puff—and reined our horses:
Rufus snorted *Doo-dah!* Saba, Pearl, and Birdy whinnied, *Go!*
So the family—siblings, in-laws, step-kin, partners, cats, macaques—
bound itself together and began to race the globe.

We shoved into the Channel. I hugged Nellie—at sweet 7, all her aunt
could dream. She sang: *Our long run stands for Us! Why keep screaming "Rat!"*
"Pig!" and "Bitch!" at one another? I stood by my younger sister as she held
her Harry—world-class toddler—on our firm foundation.
He embodied missing links from God to Nature: *Blessèd are . . . Blessèd are . . .*
Blessèd are the young, on whom we'd bet our love and money.
But Saba, the dark horse, was gone! Our cop-dog, Toby, licked
her trough. Then our Carley—halfway-grown, all lovely grace with
ponytail awave—took off and caught and raced that Bay to Rome.

Overseas, hell was hitting Gettysburg. There, our Captain sanctified
the sacrifice he'd join. As we staggered, grieving, toward the Parthenon, an oxcart
whacked my Pearl. That bobtailed nag, bucking, fell faith-first.

Lovely Emma tended her by tender lullaby: *Sandman's comin' to this babe of mine.* With the wisdom of her girl, the Babe stood up. It was 1900!

We crashed, blamed, burned, shamed, and *YA'd* our yak-drawn caravan across Ceylon on tracks of Adam, Shiva, Buddha, and St. Thomas.

Then, to every man and woman, came a moment to decide: our legs were gone! Back to Gandhi's sniping Babel—not his home for long . . .

Sweet mutt Puff fell through a mid-East crack! Ben-Hur, terrier, sobbed on Pearl—transfixed by darling Diva Daisy—pirouetting on the edge and belting, *Rock of Ages, cleft for me* . . . Birdy trotted off.

Why'd we run all day? For Henry's brilliant sciences to kindly save the wolf? For Contender Kurt to coach, with gorgeous Preludes, failing whales?

So I might cry to Natural Law, *Why not cry for me?* Why'd we race the 40s by Iron Horse—"Silver Streak"? To **BOOM** God's Law in Japanese?

Ben-Hur fell in Egypt. Toby pled; Nellie wept; I hollered; Harry slept. Great-souled Joe consoled us all: *Bronco Birdy's not long-gone!*

In Dixie, our King Reverend made our line a rugged cross. Soon, *he* was lost. Birdy sashayed home *(Oh, doo-dah day!).* Then Hell arose again.

Bearing Ben to Promised Land, stud-Rufus nudged, *C'mon!* So I shook fists at God and Nature: *Heel to me; I'm eating dust!*

2000: In Tanzania, some for each, each for some, all we beasts pulled apart, pushing on to calls of chimps: *Baby Apes! Run home!*

It was Ross and Jackson, unlikely kin like brothers, who were Gone!

We cried, *Don't cross horizons!* They shouted bravely: *But those EAGLES do!* scaring chimps into the bush. Shrieking: *TIGER!* we then sent the chimps

into the treetops, safe from tigers in the rough—where our tough explorers stood—***On your marks!***—readying to race toward any Beast—***Get set!***

And on the **B** *(Blest be . . .)* of **BANG: EAGLES! TIGERS! CHIMPS!** *(the ties that bind . . .)* **SWEET BOYS!** *(our hearts . . .)* **DON'T GO!!**

In lovely, threatened Africa, why try—*like the distant, paired macaws*—to climb a mighty fortress?—*made by flame trees, a double line, struck by sunlight into still-life torches.* Urged by flower-fire, the birds—*twin ascending, crimson streaks with tails like flags aflutter*—are singing, *US! US! US!* They won't—*we* won't—be *Us* for long. Comes a given moment and the worldwide race goes on. We're off! Heeere *we* come, by ten thousands, spinning out of a turn!

It's *our* blood—half a neck ahead of us—and half a length behind.

A length in back of that: the pack. Bound, "I" by "I," into a more-than-human chain, we cross our Dark of Heart—the home of every form of form—where countless kinds of blessèd kin fly away each day to rest forever.

Spurred by ghosts of Bach concertos pedaled out of Dr. Schweitzer's piano, we're rushing over hells of unconsciousness so deep, it's contagious—one more Monster, sprung like others out of self-erasure: denial; thought-lock; tampering; whitewash; cruelty; sleep; defeat; despair; inaction . . . We gallop down the stretch, thumping out the laws we clutch or change—transforming Us: word by cell by inch by grace along the race—*how long?*—to Be.

Dan; Sam; all of you; our new and Golden Hopes:
we'll fall, with our beasts, in the slush. Stand in for Us!

II

fair seas, a backup breeze

Growing up, the explorers told their logbooks: *Fill!*
Hockey pucks went in. Catamarans. Sweet, shaming dreams. Aids to
navigation: Kipling; Dickens; Browning . . . And prophecies of stormy ocean-
crossings they'd fulfill, like gannets over tranquil seas, by sailing back to land.
　　These darling, cocky boys needed school chums, like me,
cheering them past unacknowledged, rocking clouds of doubt.

　　Young Virgil would have fit right in—standing out—with them.
To hear them think, these port-side skippers could adapt to anything.
　　Swaying heel to heel in the suspenseful library calm,
they set their compasses by coasts already conquered in their hopes.
　　Brilliantly, they skidded through the stacks, undaunted by the clever
traps set by Evolution. It had mothered *them*, their expansive aspirations!

　　Tied, by natural habit, to the many they resembled—in ascendance,
manhood, origin—they dipped into Euripides, Shakespeare, Darwin, Freud . . .
　　Tragic flaws? Just pinpricks. Death? An antique library card.
And why check out the flops, like Walter Raleigh? Though a glance suggested
he'd been one of them—no traitor, as they'd thought. Before his execution,
he, too, had tried, in upper dark, to plumb some novel, unread stars.

On launching day, lengths of linen scooted flaglike up their masts,
joining gulls they matched. I called, *Take me? Or stay? I live for your tall tales!*
Tell me the Aleutian goose is not a threatened species! Tell me time's not fatal!

   Consoled, on the pier, by the dazzling, opaque bay, I clutched
Selected Shelley; in my hands, it overflowed with longing. I called,
Fair seas! A backup breeze! Leave your lives to find them! Don't drown trying!

The mariners made *terra incognita.* Sunlight split on wakes they rode.
Lulled by glow from wave-pit snow, they aged. Weakening, they dug up maps:
The Voyage of the Beagle; The Future of an Illusion; The Renaissance. Still,
they stalled in squalls, pitched in calms. Sextant shot, no radio, they grew old.
Had they had it? *BOOM!* They got it: *We can* move *this Odyssey!*
   With tide shifts; winds we can't predict; extra engines; bulletins . . .

Oh Captains, keep tapping back your gorgeous SOS: a signal phrased
exquisitely around the common helplessness; a link between land's ends and oceans'
meetings at land links; music's edge, outlining tides with V's of seaside sparrows;
communiqués of victory for all unbounded mains.

   Kite and crane can glide beyond Beyond—but visionary language, gliding
past a crane or kite with an age-old give and take, may unlock nature's dominance.

   Only tell us, my Tall Ship, has your wooden figurehead—
that girl who bares the breasts you've carved between her fins and wings—
pointed out the planet's rim, racing closer, closer—?

   Tell us, if you've glimpsed it, how you turned about and tacked back through
typhoons and starving octopi to constellation canopies; to dolphins who mistook you
for their own; to variegated schools of patterned dwellers in the depths.

   And how, climbing water walls along untried Great Circle Routes,
you caught fresh travelers' "MAYDAYS!"—just before they felt your tug,
and tugged back on the satin line of fragile buoys tying them
to all of the endangered—the living; dying; thriving; you.

   Then talk of every kind of friend: of "your" guillemots, how they dive
to the embrace of liquid space. And how your petrels still burst through.

12

models of comportment

He had a jones for jazz. He was white, but when he squeezed
his clarinet, the girls began to shimmy.
He did a number on that ax: the floor got hot, the boys plugged in,
and everybody shot off sparks.
His Lady Sidekick bought out all of Woolworth's Almond Joys:
no automatics, porn, or crack would ever rev *their* kids!

Harmony was hardwired in her 1970 brain. An ivory stick
in mother-rose, she loved her Big Cat like she loved the country.
She couldn't speak up loudly, or accompany off-key. With tender, right-hand
guitar strokes, this Kitty backed him up on his Grand Tour around the South.
She found a moment, unleashed an arpeggio—*zim bam boodle-oodle-oo!*—
then let her left hand strum an ancient theme—"Presentable Sex Tension"
(with modern variations)—on the body. He played along. *Go, Cat!*

The 20th Century: heading Out. Musical Liberty: old, but In:
The Constitution had a Theme with choruses and varied tones,
depending on who called himself "Interpreter" (*he* did).
His two-man band, at home in Philadelphia for a decade, belted,
Welcome, Everyone! With Improv's solo art—which spoke to all the lonely,
packed back rooms—they redid Classic Democratic Hits:
"Any Opportunity"—for the old and young; "Freedom of the Body"—
for the closeted or "out"; and, for drive-by shooters—"Rule by Rules."

Could this duo offer sweets to street-tough adolescent packs?
Enough to keep them loving jazz for long? It was teenyboppers who
revamped the dance sensations. Midlifers just flipped sizzle—*scatty wa!*—
off the griddle, praying teens hadn't split—*scatty wa!*—for R&B. Because,
to really cook, a skillet-licking Cat needed feedback that he thought no kitty
did: from kitties, crowds, kids, and Dudes—loosened not by Lindy-hops,
but by his new cool-hot rendition of the old *One-Two.*

Despite that primal bongo beat, his youth-club soon went Fusion.
Hoodlums took the hood—"One O'clock Jump" reswung—then hung boys
on clotheslines. Cops struck; the block turned over; Kitty hip-hopped
from folk-jazz toward the Big Hard Rock. How could he take the loss of face?
A flip-flop in his right hand, a flip-flop in his left, a flip-flop flew—
wa-doo!—into her rib cage. She popped him with a Kleenex wad.
As the other flip-flop sailed; she chimed, *You doo wa one more time, and I'll* . . .
(she didn't). She tapped off to *"Am I blue?"*

They stayed cordial. Measuring breaths, they snatched another decade
of the thrill of knowing no one knew which riffs would revel on what chords.
They split. Reuniting in New Orleans, his clarinet spat at her
guitar! She dipped it, dropped it, then, not to miss a beat, got down on all
fours, twanging from the floor. Tangled up in seed pearls, she couldn't twirl
his black beret. By accident, he snagged her sequin dress into a stranglehold
exposing her one pair of high-cut briefs—fire-engine red; "Victoria's Secret."
Young cats flung fat tomatoes, shrieking, *Wrestlemania's here to stay!*

The back of the Body of Law was against the wall.
Sunrise was an argument. Sunset: an argument. Midday: an assault.
While the surging masses shake their variegated ashes,
these two music lines—too finely tuned not to collide—
could compete head-on for years with nothing left between them
but tepid jungle music and cold blood.
Or, respecting their wide stretch—an L.A./D.C. separation—

each of them could improvise another solo set. And send
some stompers into space—*hootle atty wa-da!*—one more time,
on one more make-do platform.

13

anti-romantic

From day one on my '86 Chicago office run, I picked up tips,
sprinkled through our stalls: *File your beauties. Clip your truths.*
Kick your ponies, Honeys; we're off to jump the Internet. I'd been hired
to boost my youthful boss's aspirations—for roses, silver, gold.

Lunching on bruised fruit, I spent my secretary's paycheck
on trinkets I'd trade up for gems when *my* bets came in.

One day, in a minute-dodge before the copier,
my beige suede pumps were overrun by my boss's track shoes.

This beefy boy in Elvis grease called himself *Romantic—*
striving, seeking, riding human nature into pastoral sublimity.
He said he really liked me.

I divided my assignments into "Trash" and "Beauty." At the cooler,
I reported Beauty. One day, as I labored at the shredder with the Trash,
my boss, scanning Browning, said, *I'm ready for my wedge of your peach dandy.*
Clutching my paste choker, I said, *No, Sir,* brought his coffee.

I'd never worn a slit skirt, wasn't hot to trot. I'd paid before for being
chased—and I'd heard stories: *A hungry Whiz, supervising an obedient techie,*
catches an aggressive virus . . . Soon, an office non-waltz becomes a dog/fox hunt . . .

When universal Want—transfigured by Romantics—is unrequited
in someone whose strength conceals his weakness, then an underling like me,
begging off repeatedly, may meet that boss's true conviction of a rightful need.
I wasn't safe flouting such "entitlement" to me: *Take it off—or take a penalty . . .*

I tried to brush aside his quest, but even in my dreams, indignation
at injustice turned to shame at my diminishment to pain that made me sick.

If the office represented a cross section, the Sublime must leak, along
with greed, through its transactions. In fact, my gifted boss put persuasion
in a tercet: *Your Fig Newton: needa bite. / I don't get one? / I'm not nice.*

No. Your Moon Pie? No. Your Hostess Ho Ho? No. No! Then one day,
a hefty arm reached into my bathroom stall and grabbed my purse of jewels.
When I'd lost it in the tug-of-war above the door, I heard a false falsetto:
You don't need all these I.D.'s. And there, right before my feet, hightailing it
through Kleenex wads from the ladies' room, possessed by non-possession
and dead set on "Right to Git"—*track shoes!* But how could *I* escape?

Meanwhile, clouds crossed clouds. Crows wheeled home, claw by claw.

Back at his big desk, my boss gazed at me and chimed discreetly: *Chunk
of crumb cake: fork it over! On your knees,* he sighed, *for my unequal opportunity . . .*

I pled, *Illicit hounding; illegal reach-exceeding grasp.*
Behind his cactus, Track Shoes whispered, *Cream Puff—in your sixties mousse
and cherry-syrup lips!* Surely *my* human nature wasn't anything like his! But
in my sleep, a cool, Lose-Lose wind hit my fever. Soon, a twister blasted
my taskmaster—in my dreams. I woke up in a swirl of dirt that flung me,
all passivity, into the face of that man's rage—one more cold-hot collision.

I wasn't wrong. I lost my job; the boss refused me severance pay.
Tit for tat—no getaway; no finish; no replay—from any Hawthorne Track—
of our lengths of separation. He'd taken me—by my default.

15 baths a week; 10 months' halting breathing, even in my dreams.

One day, as I was breaking my gone-to-pasture streak,
I gave myself a task: *Locate your psyche in the World Wide Web. Then walk
the protest-course that the trampled often shun. Could you have sacrificed
the comfort left and leapt the net of Force and its intimidating penalties?*

Idylls gone, I'd intoned the common fearfulness—
Tap-dance off from trash, no fuss—or lose the low-wage job you need—
then lost my chance, my choice, my will, my action, and my salary.

Meanwhile, the Guy in Power lolled above us, chewing planets.

The city, stripped by storms, sighed a sigh, rhyming mine,

of shame at her shame at her dwindling expectations. And she'd lost the little beauties of her innocence: adorning buds and tendrils intimating a Sublimity beyond the odds and offices and half-composed of chaos.

Today, I've gunned my gas along a stretch of fresh-laid blacktop—
to shake those formless grabbers of my face, my form, my tail—
But the human-nature raiders, from within and from without—
have become a ravenous pack—thundering closer, closer, closer—
closing in to snatch control—stomping, tromping monster hooves
upon my unhinged skeleton.

14

bozos, bimbos, scapegoats, scum

He made us talk. Like the river—*Had it fallen in the night?*
Each day, the District turned out on the Bridge and made its call.
   When he walked by, colors streamed behind him—
a comet's tail so vivid, no one saw it split the town.
   Even We could picture his off-moments. He'd wake up afterwards
and fling himself on bimbo-mercy: *It was awesome; now I'm gone.*
   Every lapse made him, to Them, more and more, an *alien—bozo—*
thug. They accused him—*liar scum*—of midnight skinny-dipping!
   Once, that river cleared a girl the Puritans had tried
as "Satan's Bride." Just a lover thrown to rapids any witch could ride,
she'd sunk: innocent.
   A self-styled U.S. Red Guard dragged that river—for mud
to heave at *stinking enemies.* From the bottom, bobbed a Counselor
and a Blonde, with dredged-up sludge to dump upon the Commons.

We screamed *"Smear!" They* shrieked *"We've got the dirt!"*
We all stampeded through the soot; obscenities seeped through
our coats—covering, like thugs', our heads. The Law was on the lam.
   The susceptible—most of us—soon succumbed to taunting
from the nakedly gyrating, spray-slinging river-waves:
Grab the real bare-asses of your half-imagined foes . . .
   Jews, Hindus, Catholics, Muslims, Born-Agains, etc.—many faithless,

more irreverent, all became contaminated from the slime the roar had riled.

    Sleazebag thrust cuffed hands to us: *I never bruised, forced, extorted . . .*
Touch my unmalicious wrists; trust me; I need air.

    His rivals nailed his larynx, his infected sores, and his 'n' her
hard drives. Any hurt was righteous that subverted his subversion
of their pure authority. *Their* side—like scattered iron-bits,
aligned by one magnetic jolt—was completely just, like the Media.

    The Blonde advised the *slut: One smart dress will take you far . . .*
    The Counselor told her: *Let those lips that can't say "No" confess—*
or get two decades in the slammer for your Femaleness. He called her *Ho—*
her *stalker* flesh had revved the nation's pulse and stained the meat-men's
aprons muscle-pink, gut-rust, and the innocuous cream-beige
of lust. We draped the Bridge with thongs and shorts, hers 'n' his.

    Uncorking one word, "SEX"—568 times—the Counselor aroused
our taste for chaos. Eyes dilated, we were perfect witnesses: he fricasseed
the *Demon Flesh* upon the *Rule of Law.* Soon we'd eat our own.

    Some of us turned the spits that others spat upon. Some,
with snapping backs, sat transfixed. Some among us *Public—*
a bucking stallion quickly led to water—would not drink the venom-stink.

    We'd outshine the fire! So, with our faces glowing neon in the blaze,
we outwailed Israelis stuck with Palestinians stuck among Israelis.

    In public mortification dreams of Freshmen Congressmen,
Lust and Hustle, grossly swollen, wave white flags: *We've seen Paree;*
now get us home! We'll fix the general loss of grip by "doing it" with everyone.

    From the shared home—loneliness—a lone soul, ideal-struck,
had waded toward Town Meetings. But each of us believed that others
thought themselves much better (they did) and better off (they didn't).

    To make a nation, we would need some *real* representatives:
Father Scapegoat Husband Liar Devil Lover Martyr Son.

    So, through smoldering ocher shards in a witch-puce riverbed,
we dig for scraps reflecting Us. Above us, old black saints, catching whiffs
of brimstone on the charred remains of docks, lift their moonshine cups

to the whipped of recent history. Drifting down, the spirits toast:
Assimilate yourselves, your common traits.
Call your upsets "evil flukes," and they'll re-possess you!

      Sunset reclaims the sky from fire.
The colors are the same, bleeding as they cry:
Touch us, trust us, prove our substance—
then go on; do what you do:
drown in blues that drown in blues.
Suck up gold and roses.
Revel in citrines, garnets, amethysts, and emeralds: every drop
you wring from anyone.

15

when livin' ain't livin'

I know nothing about the past because I wasn't there,
and I know nothing about the present because I was there.

—Victor Klemperer

My eyes and nose are out of place in mirrors. What I call *I*
is in my mind. It shapes a present that reflects a past in which my early trust
in *Us*—Mamma, Daddy, Cynthia, Celia—inevitably called up its reverse:
distrust of *Them*. The News produced less threatening company . . .

1897. Prague: Byline, Mark Twain. **JEWS ROAST (in others' hate)**

1898. Paris: Letter to the Editor from Zola. *J'accuse . . .*

1978. With you, then my friend, I investigate the Dreyfus Case.
In self-defense, you call yourself "noncomplicitous"—by your nonexistence.
I accuse myself of human nature, and, in self-defense, ransack my delusions.
Fresh ones keep me unequipped for life's Unprettinesss.

Yet, in the stories of redemptive men and women, who transcend the
cruelties that lead, incrementally, to Cruelty, history is partially acquitted.

1900 tools along on a brilliant vehicle: people, dressed in sores
inflicted, consciously or not, by fellow bearers of contagion—human nature.

Some of us, hardly living, still get singled out for further penalties:
"they" sing, *It's a mean world till you die, with no father, mother, sister, brother . . .*

Judges rail against "their" "Negro looseness." You and I
aren't listening. Unborn, we haven't yet assumed our duty—witnessing.
We aren't informed, by the News, of lynchings, executions.

1920. Prague. Kafka: *They call Jews "Prasive plemeno" (filthy brood)*

—*Times; Sun; Globe; Mirror:* **U.S. WOMEN VOTE** *Begged 100 Years*

'21. Baptized in the Mississippi, Mamma Takes a Sip of God.
—Chicago: **DEVIL'S DANCES!** *Monkey Glide, Turkey Trot*
Bring Savagery from Africa to Clubs of Al Capone and Bugs Moran

'27. India. Gandhi: *If I were born a woman, I'd rise up in rebellion*
at anyone's idea I need permission to participate with equal liberty.
'28. **MY HUSBAND BORN (JEW) NYC** *Praise the Lord!*
'40. Amite, Louisiana: Twister Kills Mamma's Folks
'41. Dresden. Romance Languages Professor Victor Klemperer's Diary:
March: No oranges for Jews. September: No cigarettes for Jews. The omnibus
no longer may be used by Jews and only the front platform of the train. Jews must
wear the Yellow Star. November: A group of Hitler youth yells at me "A yid! A yid!"
I still hear them laughing . . . No telephones for Jews. December: Furs and woolens
must be handed over—for no payment—by the Jews . . .
'40s. *Good Germans Court and Copy Power; Drop Friends—Jews (KIKES)*
—NEGROES SINGLED OUT FOR NONINCLUSION IN THE NEWS

'41. **D.A.R. CANCELS MARIAN ANDERSON; MRS. R. RESTAGES**
—WE ENTER WAR
'42. Klemperer, June 12: *I have a strong feeling of being cast into the next*
circle of Hell by being cut off from borrowing books . . . June 13: I prepared a sheet
of paper to record the use of "blood" in all its verbal combinations . . . September 21:
On one hand, the corpses [friends awaiting deportation] *were there. On the other,*
they were really going into a beyond, from which as yet we had had no reliable news.
'40s. **HONKY TONKS TARGETED BY USA ESTABLISHMENT:**
Dangerous Crowds for Bessie, Satchmo, Billie, Duke, and Venomous Blues
'43. Klemperer Reads the News: **JEWS MENACE GERMANS**
'44. **THE NEWS: BRITS BOMB GERMANS**
~'45. Key West: Future Male Colleague, You—**All-Stars**—Join the Living

'50. Savannah: Mamma pushes me to lifelong indiscretion—my identity
'52. **JAZZ COOL;** *INVISIBLE MAN, SECOND SEX* **COME OUT**
'55. Montgomery. Wishful (White) First Edition: **BOYCOTT FLOPS!**
Goon Squads Can't Keep Coons off Bus
'60s. **ROCK HOT.** Savannah: Strong enough, from *Time* and *Life*

to bear what Mamma calls "the hope that comes when hope is gone," I'm weak enough to need it when our Life hits History in picket lines that terrify my Celia. In the kinder chaos of my mind, I find strength, hope, life, and time.

'61. Birmingham; Woolworth's Counter: **COLOREDS SIT, ASK FOR IT** *Sugar, Ketchup Poured on Heads: Harmless Fun*
—Mt. Zion Baptist: **PIANOLESS ALL-GIRL QUARTET—** **"SWEET HONEY IN THE ROCK"—HITS IT FOR THE MOVEMENT**

'63. Birmingham: **NEGRO GIRLS FIRE-BOMBED IN CHURCH**

'67. Too weak to keep cool white guys from smacking Pinpoint blacks with 2-by-4s, I still stand by the "coloreds." You march for peace in Beantown.

'70. I Marry (for Character). You claim a baseball diamond.

'72. Oval Office Tape—Nixon/Graham: **JEWS IMMORAL BASTARDS!!**

'75. Chi-town: Though No One, I fight cruelty to Carla, Raul, Blacks . . .
—Big Apple: *Cynthia Defends, Big-Time, the Singled Out for Penalty:* A Tapper; A Tennis Champ; An Anchorman; The Hurricane; You 'n' Me, Sister . . .

'85. Ms. Freespeech, a conflicted blonde with clout to spin Sin City Roulette Wheels, sends you, via News, from the Minors to the Major Leagues.

'86. La La Land: Reflected in your media crowd, I—a No One/ Docudramatist—am *I*—by my unlikenesses! In Savannah, I speak up for Celia.

✦ ✦ ✦ ✦ ✦

A DOCUDRAMA: ACT I

'93. Surf City: You, new Network Host, give me raves; deny me raises, call, spring to fall, *Look what I got* Us! Phantom girls chime, *Like Old Times!*

'94. Good old friend Kool Gent, 1 of 3 state-paid writing-screeners, tells me, *It's* my *job to give* you *routine treatment—just give* me *Satisfaction!*

    I: *If I start you up to get professional consideration, what will that make me?*

    KOOL GENT: *Ho?? No! You'll be "Chick for Free"—beneath my thumb.*

    I: [32 MONTHS LATER] *To your 5 no-context propositions, bald-faced "I Want Candy's" with no reference to me, I had every right to say, "Sorry, No."*

    K.G.: *I tried and I tried . . . Your kindness means you owe me. Send pages . . .*
[his rejection, 10 DAYS LATER] *"Till you hold me like I say, you're OUT!"*

I: *Cynthia and my husband back me up: Anywhere the Law applies, NO ONE—* *no WOMAN—with any facts or attributes, may be singled out for unearned penalty.*

LADY FREESPEECH: *Yes! Speak! You got soul (and my control). GO!*
YOU: *Hush, Little Babe. You've got too much; negotiate! You asked for it.*
I: *With 3 years' courteous "No"? Who'd request a blackball? He'd reviewed* *me—"a female Whitman/Stevens"—then forced on me 4 types of "lesser treatment."*
Even if I seem to be a brat, Madonna, Venus, Honky Tonker, almost–Ivory Girl, *I belong to me. "Exaction-or-Retaliation's" outlawed—or any buddy, boss, squeeze,* *1-night-stand, sidewinder, shark—any stronger wannabe—can say, "Lady lay—or pay."*
YOU: *Harmless fun. Brothers-in-Arms do not cheat weaker chicks!* [exit]
K.G.: *I'm not sorry; why the fuss? Be honored by the compliment!*
I: *I bled; you said, "It's nothing. Let it bleed." I'm hemorrhaging! I'm not the* *undisputed worst, but this "least treatment's" not a first. I'm nothing!* [K.G. exit]
LADY: **I'll help—with inside info.** *Shake it, Baby! Rattle! Roll!* [exit]

LADY [reenter with K.G.; point at me]: You've *made me "Faithless Love"* *to his trusting folks—my friends. You* made *me help you; I must make it up to them.*
I: *His folks are well, you say, and not involved. For two long years, I begged;* *he stonewalled. If I leave, he strong-arms on. It's gratuitous and not uncommon!*
LADY: *Fox,* I *never got a hunt; you ask for it, so shut up! It's no win!*
I: *But if that bus called "Sex or Else" don't stop now, inch by inch,* *sparing natural women who've upheld this Field that's diamond-cut, then when?*
LADY, GENT IN SYNC: *Don't be crool [go away]. We'll control you* *[it's all over]. Baby Blue, yakety yak, AND WE'LL PAINT YOU BLACK!!*
May '97. Mamma Dies. Aided (Cynthia, Pamela), I carry on my case.
Jan. '98. *K.G.'s Home Court Flags His Plays: "DISCRIMINATION"* *TIME HAS COME TODAY TO RUN FOR LIFE. Little Girl.*

ACT II

'90s. NYC Courts; THE NEWS: **BLACKS, GAYS, OLD WIN 8 OF 10**
Slandered by Co-Workers for Their Bosses, Women Win Just 2 of 10
'98—[**Flogging Room,** *Crazy* Diamond-Cut] 1st Base: I. 2nd: LADY.
3rd: YOU. Infield: 3 TIPS; 6 PAC. Sidelines: ROCK & RAP (Dad & Son)

[deadpan, all take four steps left, four right, four left, continuously]

LADY [to stands]: I'm *like* you, *a patriot. But "Tupelo Honey"* [point at 1st] *used us for her dirty work.* [dip] *That Jury didn't buy my slurs!! Mirror Mirror, from the "PRIVILEGED INFO" K.G. slipped me, twist new curses!* **[sing for years]**

She's *the devil in disguise!* [double dip; point at 1st] *At a* **Private Hearing,** *she lied to hide evil, vile UGLINESS* [kick] *of A FEMINIST!!* **[KICK]** *Pass it on!*

THE 3 (Beef) TIPS: *That Cookie* [point at 2nd] *cuts sluts* [point at 1st] *who pack sledgehammers in slit skirts. Mercy! But* [dip to 2nd] *she's a Lady.*

LADY [to stands]: *EAT BLIND RAGE: SHE'S A BITCH!* **[KICK]**

I: *Lady's made-up cruelties to a Beast of Burden—me—whom she's blamed since I won—to justify the shameful mud she slung—were* all *she heard that day.*

YOU: *(Lady speaks the truth when boosting* me . . .*) Those little girls' thunder road means a hard rain's gonna blow our minds, noses, and control. Mercy!*

I: *Deacon Blues, you're still 7 stories tall, our champion Yanks—whose Laws free all—even this rule-honoring Romantic—from being traded for a chance.*

TIPS: *You must have heard, Mockingbird* [point at 1st]—*shut up!* [dip] *Like adored tradition, our force is irresistible. Anytime, anyhow, you* have gotta give!

I: *At that 8-hour forum like 1,000,* his peers *called "HALT." That's all.*

I'm *the one* **who NIXED the ax** *he'd get for losing fights with Law! I champion you, Prince Hitters, who don't strip and spread—want to?—to be read like everyone. Spared your cohorts' sex-extortion, you don't see the cruelty.*

LADY [to stands]: *THE SLUT HAS SPAT ON JUSTICE!* **[KICK]**

YOU: *Scamp, why aren't you off somewhere blinking at a star?*

I: *I am. Tapes and records prove my aim is true!* **It's still** your *beautiful field— absorbing a broad base! Enchantment pours from open doors! Who's asking for equality? Outside, I'm praised; Inside* [twist] *I'm sacked!* [shout] *U2, Shoo-Pac?*

6 (Shoo) PAC [point at 1st]: *Ruby, Ruby, with Dude Process, you out-dood a Dude. You stole our rib, you asked for it, & you make blamin' cool.* [grab ROCK.]

ROCK: *I did* not *kill Jazz!* [to RAP] *Rock on, Son!* RAP [hug Dad]: *Mercy!*

LADY: *STRIP MS. PIECE OF TAIL! MANE TO TWAT! GOSSIP!*

I: *It's not a gas to send word-up—"I'm not bartered property!"—just to find crazy, grape-vine CRUELTIES that CONTROL me—WITCHY WOMAN— by a fantasy dismantlement, leaving me in tatters from colleagues' "harmless" fun.*

With what offense—autonomy?—have I "asked for" this punishment?
I'm fair game again!
    LADY: *A BULLSEYE FOR THE RIGHTEOUS!* [KICK HER OUT]

    GIRLSOUND: *They'll drive Rival Dixie down.* [twang] *Laughing—pass it on.*
    FIELD [reel]: *Rock, go! Everybody must be stoned! Filly Freedom, duck!*
    DIAMOND [on soles]: *Chain Lightning* [flash] *strikes The Chasm!*
    TIME and LIFE [strobe take over]: *Everybody, skip the light fandango!*
    YOU [slide IN]: *Lady Sans Merci, why buck Us? Shut up and recant!*
    I: *I can't! I've spared you floods I wept! I ain't too proud to beg!*

    YOU [high in cheering stands] and I [OUT in no-man's-land]
[both point; sing as one]: *I Got You, Babe.* [bow]

[POWER FAILURE]

✦ ✦ ✦ ✦ ✦

'98–. Bleeding, broken, I holed up with my husband, calling, *Mamma!*
They got me!—a piece of nut-tomato cake served up on false witness at a door
shored by folklores and other mental buttresses. Better mugged and muzzled!

    Yet I knew: *I'm meeting it; now the old devil has once more got his spine*
through the waves . . . Reality, so it seemed, was unveiled . . . I had a satisfaction
in being matched with powerful things, like wind and dark [Virginia Woolf]—and
negation, defamation, and the smug exclusion of the weak by the strong,
who count upon and receive their sympathy. (*She* 'got' no feeding frenzy!)

    But the hangman couldn't rid the Court of witnesses: Zola, Twain,
Kafka, de Beauvoir, Holiday, Ellison, Stern—or Klemperer's saving argument:

    We've so much loved each other, I'm not sure it's going to end. It's not only
the word "impossible" that's out of circulation; "unimaginable" has also lost validity.

    Yes, I'm No One—but for loved ones, the grace of whose reflections
lets me live. And for that Jury's Verdict—standing up like Handel's
Oratorio: *Live forever, Solomon!* The outcome, based on typical, if surprising
facts—cruelties that I'm driven to half-tell, and that I have half-lived to tell—

was for *someone*—no one but myself, **inch by inch:** a reliable narrator. And it was a judgment for a Many (never One): islands of applause and accusation with the separate mountain majesty of greed; hate; need; love; of me 'n' you—Brother.

1999. The Big Easy: **STREET JAZZ THREATENED**
Church Zones Ban Pianos, Clarinets
THE NEWS: BEHIND BACKS IN OUR FACES, TIME NABS LIFE
You and I, evading conflicts—The Dominant v. The Denied—that neither side has won for long, have staggered to a border boarding house: A.D. 2000 U.S.A.

From our window, we've glimpsed a pair of arms,
extended from the window of an unknown, nearby building.
"Who was it? A friend? A good man? Someone who sympathized?
Someone who wanted to help? Was it one person only? Or was it mankind?"—

whose face, misplaced in our brains,
we failed to recognize.

16

transfusion

For saints have hands that pilgrims' hands do touch.

—William Shakespeare, *Romeo and Juliet*

Louis talks with Jimidee, raging speechlessly upon two pillows;
with Evaly, a passive stretch of flesh; and with Professor Crown, who points
to letters on a board to talk. "W-A-L-K" is out, but he can push his wheelchair
to his D-A-U-G-H- . When she leaves, he sinks into a Stephen Hawking dream:
a Giant Star trades its radiance with the fading reds of dying Dwarfs.
    • When the Big Top stopped in Georgia—'61—I left the freaks,
the cats, and trapeze acts to circle, in the sawdust, all of them.
    Meanwhile, young Louis, "Souie Louie" to New Orleans bullies,
wouldn't eat his rice—to honor starving kids and thwart his mother.
A few years later, Evaly had graced our college stage with dance. I caught,
in the audience, the flush that fired exquisite bronze: her face, legs, arms.
    Meanwhile Louis, a large, pale man called "sissy," seldom "masculine,"
signed up—Trauma Nurse—for Nam, came home a Majordomo for the Gone.

Jimidee, 20—called "Straight Dope" before the Monster bit his flesh—
yanks away his air-tube, breathing, *Hallelujah!* I sit beside Professor Crown,
who dozes, wakes, grips my knee, and spells out ITHACA. Is he Ulysses,
kidnapped in his sleep to an alien beach where he cries out for home?
    Louis rents this space. Strong, he shops for produce, 5:00 A.M.,
for "Broth du Jour" for his weak patients. *I* came sliding to his hospice on
Chicago's icy streets. Like Robert Scott, on his last expedition, I had thought,
"My ponies' hooves are split; there are signs of unseen ringbone . . ."

Beside my silent Evaly, I "tap" *her* "recollections":
Interpreting for Alvin Ailey with my arms and legs, I gave up hating my behind . . .
Jimidee tosses me a dashboard ornament, rasping in Kentucky tones,
I need a sweet Madonna, dressed in rhinestones on a pedestal of abalone shell . . .

Evaly sings back! *Pallas Athena Thea. Akoué!* (Praise!) *Akoué! . . .*
It's a hymn we sang as freshmen on the Bryn Mawr Library steps!
She's bled again. Louis packs her womb with gauze. I "reenter"
her near-past: *Some stranger's ramming hate into my flesh . . .*
Louis diapers Mister Crown—who's unabashed at that, having shed
his British accent, 3-piece suit, formality. Now, he doesn't ask if he deserved
to study literature. For decades, he had beat his brains on "errors" in his essays,
in his character. Letting-up—at 66—the pounding merely demonstrated he was
made of flesh—which he'd hated in proportion to his laborings after goodness.
Jimidee can't doo-dah in the bedpan.
Evaly's still singing: *He's a wino. He's sublime-o. For some young thing*
from Shipley, divine-o . . . That's "Haverford Harry" ("the boy that I marry")!

It's the Unconscious coming out, with the wisdom of the stripped.
Professor Crown spells his response to Shelley: *We dared the dragon*
from its den—"Cold Death for One by One by One." *We'd all heard it whimpering.*
Louis swabs red flesh around Crown's food-tube. Then he hints, gently,
that it's useless. He tells me what he's witnessed: instant blindnesses in wives
who saw their husbands shredded by Khmer Rouge scythe-machetes.
I bang my head on pebbles slung at me—*"bitch cruel slut malicious stupid*
piece of ugly flesh bad dog bimbo ugly witch"—then take the spoon from Louis.
But Evaly is closed. Like the hate that closed her, she's untranslatable.
In our continuous exchange, I'd called her my "Snow Leopard"—had I
sensed a threat? Wouldn't many hate us for the love we called our friendship?
Louis reinserts the air tube into Jimidee's splotched face, then makes

his round around the cots. He tops off everybody's "Crème de Glucose."
Coughing for attention, John Crown plays, with startling eloquence
and his habitual grace, his final part: "A Pardoned Man, Pardoning."
He gasps: "*If my heart were great, 'twould burst at this.*

Captain I'll be no more, but I will eat and drink and sleep
As soft as Captain shall. Simply the thing I am shall let me live—"
I'm Evaly's "Black Swan," but I only thrash my thoughts: *I've never*
slandered anyone. Or robbed, hit, taunted, backstabbed, used, abused, abandoned . . .
"All's Well" ends. Then our Professor's flesh turns blue—crumpling
as if fired upon. His left eye shuts; his right is frozen open, one month more.
And did the stones God dropped upon him
give his essays weight?

Has some miraculous transference taken place
that I, who've so loved others, I almost thought I *was* them, who now
dodge almost everyone, am offered tender hospice alongside the departing?
I've stood up to a few, saluted many . . .
It's Louis who'll be wakened, like Ulysses by Athena, with the News:
Akoué! You're in Ithaca. Akoué!
But first, it's Evaly who must be washed, braided, blessed,
wept for, laid out, wept and wept for . . . Across her breasts, I rest her arms:
arms I couldn't clasp, in mid-trajectory, to fling her—spinning, flying—back
into the high suspense of continuity. I couldn't trade her flesh and mine.
Why can't I do Communion right? I'd lift us all to higher ground,
but I can't even raise my eyes. I only stare, dizzy, nauseous, caught in fever's snare . . .

Even as he regroups in the hall, our Captain, Louis,
gathers us. Next to me, our Jimidee holds my hand and hums.
In my fantasy, we freshman girls still sing. I'm swinging
the class lantern. All together, we proceed: *Sister, help to trim the sail . . .*

Louis, row your load of souls ashore.

part **III**

I must hide in the intimate depths of my veins.

—Léopold Senghor

Memory would come like a rope let down from heaven to draw me up
out of the abyss of not-being, from which I could never have escaped by myself.

—Marcel Proust

Then—watch the roses, notice how they move,
their gestures are so minuscule
they would be imperceptible but that
the rays diverge and fill the universe.

—Rainer Maria Rilke

17

winged bike

Transfixed by the glimmer of the pale blue air on dense blue sea,
he had no grasp of the Beyond and couldn't fathom the Beneath.
He listened; all he heard
quickly joined the blur of a baffled, distant murmur.

Some receptacle he was, spilling what he caught!
In 7 years, he learned to walk.
9 more, and he was ideal-struck; he could hardly run.
Too shy to sing at 20, he'd think, *Sublime,* call, *High notes!*
He met his Delta Princess, and Swing became his vehicle.
Fluttering with common gulls, they tangoed Georgia's coast.
Crying out, *Big Bands!* he meant, *Don't drop the driving beat!*
One January, ankle-deep in foam from the Beneath, they married.

Drawn by the Beyond—and boat, plane, train—to Rio, Cairo, Kyoto,
they ambled banks like those expanding Rome and Amsterdam. Each
composed librettos to transcend his partner's melodies, then went past
words and met his match: the other. Then, from defensive trenches, each,
by the other, got reprieved. When Hard Love kicked them far enough,
they paused in disbelief: their regrets had marched in step for decades.
When their hopes, rapid-like, evaporated, other wellsprings sprang:
texts as old as hooded cranes; Schönberg; Ives; the mind's winged bike . . .

One May day, in her waltzing-Togo caftan, she vanished—
from June, July, August . . . Just-lost, she couldn't soothe the coming losses.
Her face—though not her loveliness, which wasn't why he'd loved her—
grew faint and yet consoled his soul—which loveliness still touched.

76. Mid-River: A canal lock, enfolding a despair-hold. Suddenly,
his wails sailed up, splitting pairs of geese—who need to hear each *other* sing.
Then when, by transistor, he heard an Air Force Band go down
with its Pacific carrier, he sang, *andante,* too: *Carry me, Sweet Chariot*—stopping

short to beg: *Another movement! An allegro!* Let it make reality Perfection!
But every heightened instant, elusive as a quark, became a target
for the second-guesses striking, every other second, his hard-stricken heart.
All at once, a corridor emerged. Abloom—flute-green—inside his head,
it headed upward! He'd tool through by Starlite Coupe and skid home just
in time—for turning 79! High-stepping with the pelicans in wave-spray, he'd
clutch each moment—looming over all the others it would pulverize . . .
Then *another* moment, rolling on its rush, would crash down hard and crush it.

81. He listened: a *Hush* met that murmur from Beyond. It was just
the song of a nova, pulsar-bound: *Play, Little David, on your harp!*
Beneath: caves, cliffs, canyons—ordered into Being till they vanish on
command: lands hard-reached by rowboat on the oceans they'd been lost in
since the eons formed the coasts that would be lost without
the tides, a system circulating to its satellites—moons soon lost without
the planet that's beneath them and beyond. Our Father Earth holds
tight for life all his kids—*Hallelu!*—despite lifelong discomfort with life's blood.

Just before the roses on the Georgia coast nod off,
and eucalyptus leaves toss the afternoon's last glitz to evening's mist,
July, November, all the months take wing for the Unseen. He's listening.
It's almost time—*how long?*—for Time to fly him into the Sublime.
Finally, he'll realize that ideal stratosphere—just beyond the ancient, hard
expanse of aspiration. He'll join the chains of particles sprung from planets'
shifting cores and free-form hearts of stars, then linking up within a fog
of infinitesimal strings, twanging with dark energy . . .

He'll take that dance-pulse (60 beats per minute)
in his—in *everybody's*—wrist, just until the minute
he stops listening to Imagination's tune:

    Play me through:
I'll play with you;
my counterpoints will yank you down, then shove you up
against a blue you think you'd bleed to love—
that always loves another blue.

18

altars in the urban heart

I'm not in hiding, only people-shy.
Sometimes I go out, heart open,
hoping nothing slams it shut.

Years ago, he entered it, with his black-pool eyes,
his hair that wouldn't lie down flat,
his mouth that so confounded me, I kissed it for an hour at a time.
Of all our no-job crowd, he had the most to say, was the most
inclined to silence. He suffered from the cold and from uncertainty:
what other cruelties would come along and make him ache?
My footsteps in his shadow never drew a word from him,
and when he stretched his hands for chords, he hardly glanced at his guitar,
but fixed his gaze in space as if on everything he wanted.

He had something—he just wasn't certain it was "something."
In the condemned assembly hall on Stony Island Avenue, and only
when his audience of strays in street-smart clothes—to show assurance—
had gone, he'd play his violin. He'd *become* his violin.
Every day I hear his strokes upon those strings again,
a fantasy that coexists with a different wish:
Don't let me dream of anyone, or let another fill me so completely,
I'm nothing but a dream of him.

Leave me with no comfort in this white-on-black Chicago,
with her snow-choked roadways that no one can pass upon.
Leave me no one, though no one can live through winter here
with no other soul to touch, if only in a dream.

I might have spent 10,000 nights beside him.
Wrecking balls that swung from Sandburg Village to Cabrini Green
put him in a trance. Envisioning himself before the window of a tenement,
he saw a two-ton sphere arcing toward his demolition. After
he snapped out of it, he'd lift his clarinet and toast: *To high notes!*
Smiling with closed eyes, he'd hold each high note like a kiss
with no future in it.
Accidents and illness picked upon our generation.
In a Hyde Park rehab, noting on my calendar the bankruptcies
and breakdowns of old friends, I waited for his crosstown call.
Twice a year: *Are you all right?*
Are you?

Oh, to show the commonness of the common talent—or to prove his *gifts,*
which he dismissed. He, who coaxed sonatas from his keyboard, horn, and piccolo,
and hardly noticed flaws in compositions like my own.

The troubadours who'd strolled South Shore, our former haunt,
have disappeared. Deer, raccoon, and gangs,
starved out of their habitats, have moved into the suburbs.
I hear we've lost another chum: an airplane crash.
My thoughts career. *Who's equipped for self-defense from thunder clouds?*
I imagine bone-bits of that tagalong
suspended in the sky like debris in an explosion,
his moment come to show what he was made of.
From my knees, my laptop drops.

Driven from the house by its inhabitant, myself,
I seek that instrumentalist from whom I still refuse to be removed:
He's punishing the piano in his club on 47th;

he makes the keys concede;
he bends the room with beauty.

> *And if he'd never said to me, if only in his sleep,*
> *"God I better get away from you"—*
—we might have had 10,000 nights.

> It's the bite of lack of confidence—how deep it dug, what veins
it struck—
that makes his jazz magnanimous.
And given shrines like this to bridge *all we want*
and *what we get,* at least we'll have some music.

> 15 minutes peace on the Electric Train, then I'm alone
in a giant tunnel. Shadows of old friends march by,
waving, calling, drowning out the train, the city, everything but
How can I get over my first love, his lips still warm from his harmonica?

> If I could peel away bad luck and bury it on Maxwell Street,
I'd dance naked on the frozen lake.

> In my head, there's whispering:
> *Love was made for caves. But in a tougher neighborhood,*
> *love is less like something extra; love is more like Love.*

> How much I'd have missed if I hadn't followed him
through gaps in chain-link fences
into the bare back lots, where, between the two of us,
we almost had enough.

19

in no time

I've crossed a room to meet a man I've read about in *Life*.
We chat. In no time, I'm swimming in his light.
He matches my attention. I'm transparent.

At 17, I gave too much devotion:
I'd do anything where have you been who are you . . . ?
I had no defenses. I had feelings for Prince Myshkin in an instant.
Generous, sensitive, he threw himself to love—and proved he was
"The Idiot." Stupefied, he witnessed love's undoing of his sanity.
Page by page, I rushed, enthralled, to him in his oblivion,
bringing all he'd drawn—more love—uselessly, from me.

Since then, and even when I like someone—everyone—
I've become more careful.
I'm composed: of friends; kin; husband.
So look at me! Nakedly transfixed by an author
who has shaken me, who's shaped me with his eloquence,
who gives events, with his largesse, resonance;
who's glancing at my blouse, mouth, knees—

Suddenly, from nothing, specks of color overspread, dumbfoundingly,
my blank, interior picture screen. They generate a labyrinthine undergrowth
whose triple scarlet blooms begin bursting in delirium from ordinary white ones . . .

Though paralyzed, at 25, by my unmet demands,
I nearly swooned on meeting Prince André in *War and Peace.*
    It wasn't just his personal force that jolted me,
but nothing less or more than his correctly measured character!
    That love was "human," was, for him, no excuse for anything
but insight, hindsight, foresight, and omniscience.
    And passion, was it Passion, given those heroics?

    It's over 7,000 days since then. I've met up with less-than-love:
at times, as overwillingness; at times, as an exacting will
whose clutch has crushed me deaf—dumb—numb.
    A look, a little talk, and this reliable idealist—
who's stirred me for a decade by commanding grand confoundments,
is waking me, once more, with such an unconfused magnetic tug,
I think he has a core of iron, silver, gold, platinum . . .

    Ivory garlands drape an island, where, in hushed uproar, the violet vines
that stroke the beach unleash a boat for two, who row into the blue on blue
until the haze gets lost in mist that spills from thunderclouds it filled . . .

    That daydream was my doing! But at my unruliest, I was no Lizaveta,
heroine of *The Possessed*—dispossessed of all her equilibrium.
    My hard-won solidity's dispelled my family's worries. Now, although
I'm undone in one fellow's princely gaze, my history of illumination
by a few extraordinary men can rebegin. A different form of Beauty—
with the usual romance—has made its old breath-taking sense.
In no time, Love is news again.

    My flower-pit, where blossoms start in sweetness,
had remained, in spite of life, unstained!
    I return his kind good-bye,
then seize, before I lose the chance, a last, delicious glimpse.
    This man's no one's but his own imaginative masterpiece.
    He stands, not unyieldingly—someone who may never
altogether leave my mind—

and steps forever out of reach.

I picture, as he goes, a shining midpoint on a line connecting, from within, the two sides of his head:

Center of grace,
Center of gravity—
joined in him, centering me.

20

venus as a ship's light

A travelogue: *And away we go . . . !*

Once your cautious student, I grew rash, took on passion.
Loneliness unleashed my wildness on your solitude.
After that, we sprung romantic phrases
within a fixed form: marriage. Each of us reached with words
to the other, who reached back. We shunned the other opiates—
gambling, drugs, ambition, love—to keep from risking Love.
Gaucho-like, you'd galloped into my imagination, spearing
golden rings—desire, devotion, hope . . . You *still* read my reveries.
Look! Someone's filling up my inner movie screen . . .

It's Percy Shelley—recast as James Dean! And there I am,
resembling me, escaping from the Present in black leather.
It's *my* vehicle; I'll hitch a ride. Dean's become a trucker,
pulling over to the shoulder of this daydream. I hop in.
Rebel, Rebel of the worldwide fantasy, he's daring me desirously:
Eat my speed and be like me—the long-lost "Avant Garde"! I spark! Our 18
wheels catch fire! Before I blaze, the rig explodes! I'm thrown to Purgatorio.
I toss sweet nothings home, Sweetheart, then vault into Inferno—
the bottom hold of a slave ship boiling near Galapagos.

This isn't physical; it's metaphoric. Look! A bigger wish—"Save Thy Neighbor." Rosier than Mars, it rises in my inner space. But it's a futureless illusion, hit by ruthless and entrenched competition. Hurtling like Mercury, it tips my ship—my *psyche*. Hair aswirl, I'll drown in hate. *Darling: "SOS."*

But who but me can read me? Or row, with the recklessness of thought, my unfit Lifeboat—*me?* Who but me is heading head-on into No Emotion? It's a rock-ice, stone-soul Pole! My mouth has frozen shut.

Turn about—break the lockhold! Then—oh blessèd—from my throat: *drop, drop*—melting sweat! *Feeling! Verbs! Imagination! Flow!*

✦ ✦ ✦ ✦ ✦

Dante placed Desire beside *Amore*—and 28 enchanting rhymes for it. On *my* Romantic plank, *Ms. Temperate Zone,*—I floated on. *(How long?)* Suddenly, Venus shone, as low upon Tierra del Fuego as another ship! My metaphor projected her, down from out-of-reach to be dream-company.

Human correspondents, too, sent reflections: altered states, feeding me civilization's calm *(though my old gang's contagious frenzy rages on).*

And Dante's Love—that turns, my Love, the sun/planet/star roulette— still transported us beyond Beyond. I saw myself anew: connected.

(I'd expected only what's due All). Darwin, back at home in London, glimpsed, in epiphanies, the meaning of the finches on his trip: Evolution's absolute requirement for variety. My risks, too—a grasp exceeding reach, retreat, flagellation, flight (back, forth, forth, back), adapted to my insights, from letters, all types. Bound, grounded, classic, personal, off-the-press, aloft:
. . . these birds flutter to rest in my tree . . .
I have heard them saying,
"It's not that there aren't other worlds, but we like this one best."

It's our doubled space, whose gate swings out or in; where chariots of flesh and speech lift the Real sublimeward. Where Id and Ego—Psyche's Favorite Picture Shows— exchange their ever-changing sense.

And as the petals of flowers in falling waver and seem not drawn to earth,
So he seemed over me to hover light as leaves
And closer me than air. And music flowing through me
Seemed to open mine eyes upon new colours . . .

Carissimo, you worry:
What the hammer? What the chain?
I've replied, *A Tyger's tools to pry—from all extremes—at nature's secrets . . .*
Ask me: *In what furnace was thy brain?* And I'll sing—surviving,
driving, standing, reaching, waving through my moonroof, almost home—
The one that heats my blood, churning meaning into images
I'm sending you, from Whitman Bridge, by ancient rebel song:
"Awake, O North, and come, O South.
Blow upon my garden that its spices may flow out . . ."

21

the solace of the possible

What's attractive, apart from the jazz, is how his postcards
leave me guessing his next destination, not where I stand with him.
    What a lovely back he has! He also has a lot to say,
records it now and then. Like me, he improvises.
    I can easily imagine that he has a wife in Canberra, a girlfriend
in Milan. What I have for him is a passion worth reentering.
    This study of that love, which takes place in my head,
won't heat up anybody's blood.

    Behind the scenes, I do all the living that I can.
I've translated treatises on modern dance from Japanese,
and I have a husband who, when we watch the Evening News, rests
his head upon my hip and fills me with such tenderness, there's no room
for the government. I don't have to say my name to hear it spoken
with affection. And, in winter, waking to the robin's-egg-blue paint
upon my windowsill, I reliably envision
the hydrangea-blue sky of a summer afternoon.

    There's nothing strange in loving what one sees in the imagination's
intermittent light—a many-tinted mix: needs; wishes; recollections; chaos . . .
    When a former upperclassman, who had traveled Africa by clarinet,
returned to Philadelphia, it wasn't only in a public spotlight that I saw him . . .
    Standing in the doorway of his master class, I was 1,000 fans.

Who wouldn't wish to give such adoration? Back at home, I guessed
his height and then the depth of his disconsolation, mentioned casually.
Then I caught the undertow of reverie, catching me . . .

One person's long immersion in another: call it *Love*? I've heard
tales of pitfalls of false passion. Yet my story of non-intimacy with this
instrumentalist offers, in the end, no regrets, only gratitude that I, who'd once
been frightened by upholstery, was nurtured by abstractions—Imagination;
Memory; Him—as sensual as music, swirling visibly into my living room.
   True, those lovely eyes of his were hardly my creation. And it was
a shock of hair, falling on his forehead like a bird's tail, that remained
so clear, long after lost from view, it always overcame me with emotion.

Keep in touch, he'd called, not meaning something tangible.
I dragged "him" back to my existence, kept him—handsome, brilliant—there,
took the role of witness, not forgetting fans' demands, nor my protectiveness,
nor other difficulties he was—*I* was—up against, heard from him by phone
from Paris, 3 months later, 2:00 A.M., pleased, for once, with a performance.
   People tell me passion is a matter of fragility. Certainly it was desire
that routed my defenses. But I'm not taking on the flesh's frailty; my theme
is merely Longing, a force that can be pounded into power in the brain.
   When my gaze got lost in his, I pictured the magnetic waves
of physics: unseen, ruffling nothing, they envelope everything. That's
potency! Objects, with their glorious materiality, are almost ineffectual.
   Granted, two dejected lines, scribbled on his Canada Itinerary,
brought to mind the 12 uses of "desire" in "Venus and Adonis" . . .
   Do only *paltry* passions demand elaboration in interior reflection?
Mine's enveloped me so all-embracingly, I've needed no embraces!
I've even told the image I call "him," *You'll be no less substantial if you go!*

Why shouldn't *I* be otherwise, and require no lockhold
on a semi-stranger unattuned to my attention to him?
Why expect some unessential proof of our attachment?
   Yes, I've subjected him to every sweet nothing I've ever conjured up,
but in my most audacious dreams, I've only—now and then—kissed him.

When fantasy carries me beyond my expectations,
I'll wrap a leg around him.
Cut! Scene complete!

     Best to just project him onto my cerulean ceiling. He gets so bright,
he blurs, merging with my husband! Or each becomes two men, and I'm
the version of myself I like, absorbed by passion too sublime to redirect itself
onto the fabulous reality of actions: it hurtles to the blazing pit of thought.
     And I can live on compact discs, since, behind my eyes, light becomes
a bell, drum, elephant, or, summoned in from Zanzibar—hands in pockets,
standing on his heels—this masterpiece. Who'd give him up? Who wouldn't
choose the solace of the Possible within the broad sweep of what's not?

     If only I could listen to his whole improvisation! Each time I read
his mind, I notice that he's carried off, like I am, by contemplation of his own
heart's griefs and compensations. I can easily imagine how he'd lift his face,
drop his eyes, and slide them sidelong to meet mine.
     And I, who re-create myself for this man whom I remake;
and to whom I'm still so drawn, I weep each time I play the tapes
on which his gifts *(touch; drop; fly; shift . . .)* far exceed musicianship;
and whom I can't define because, in heating up my blood,

he rarefied my life with a version of Exquisite that's my idea of Ideal,
I'd let my phantom hands barely brush his phantom face,
and my sadness, meeting his, would become *our* hopefulness,
and compound my feelings, and return them, and affirm
the solitary shortcut through the continents I'd take again and call it Love—
     I'd tell him, *When you go,*
you'll leave these walls as azure blue as on that evening
you came dancing through them.

22

the stretch

12/1/2000, 7:00 A.M.: There's Yael, bobbing down the ice, jacket flapping.
In sunlight off our slanted roofs, her lovely face is gem-set
in a cowl neck. She's taller—all at once!—than next spring's lilacs. She turns
the heads of skinny wrens, pecking snow. Out of my front window,
I see them turn again: Elizabeth, her no-less-lovely mother, catches up.
You—6'1" (but taller); 72 (but younger); half-blind in foggy glasses—
divine your way into that sidewalk scene.
At 41—to my 19—you'd swept me up with chamber music:
fantasies for flutes and drums. Now and then, we had ideas:
On a pinpoint, Here, bonded to an instant, Now, you and I are bound
for There and Then—where, again, we won't stay long. And each of us—
You, I, Here, Now, There, Then—is homeless (less significant) alone.

South window: a cardinal is bowing to the ghost of honeysuckle.
Flashback: World War II, your college years:
A La Recherche du Temps Perdu retrieved you from your battle shock.
Later, I got stuck inside *my* jungle.
Pulling, from your black kit bag, armfuls of ideal forms,
you sprung my booby traps. After that, I promised you:
With tunes (Johannes', Ludwig's, Amadeus's) that you'd sung since
junior high, you and I would seize the day from Mind and Nature . . .
Mayday! You've crashed into a leaf pile left from fall!

Rushing to an eastern window, I cry mutely: *Rise my love, my fair one;*
come away . . . then notice, at *his* window-perch across the street, Mr. Wong,
imprisoned in his gently twisted form, smiling, waving, *Do not be afraid!*

To the western traffic-buzz—a form of silence, with a backdrop (one
more form of silence) of melodic medleys, weaverbird to rock dove, finch,
and starling *(Twee, twee, plee . . .)*—you read *Der Untergang des Abendlandes*
(whew whew whit whit whit . . .). In your shadow *(Apple tree among the trees . . .),*
I collect my quarks, wobbling north toward the Hermans' all-birds' sanctuary.
Outlaw squirrels have spun from wise, young Ari's crunch on not-white
sidewalk under not-black trees that defend our line of homes—
    pillars of smoke out of wilderness. At the Strausses': John Drazenovic ascends
a ladder lent him by our brave-heart veteran, George Benjamin. Mrs. D.
sees summer gold inside the stripped forsythia. John Coruthers hums along,
blowing snow to heaven. *The Idenos moved to Skokie; who'll leave popcorn out*
in baskets for the gods? Where's Corporal Willie, long since home from Nam?

    In our enclosed garden, I rub numb hands; there I am: 1961; Hattiesburg,
Mississippi, waking up with Ellen, 5 (not yet FBI), to my Roblyn's shoofly pie
and our Granny's whisper-song: *Rise up and give God your Glory, Glory, Glory!*
    Yesterday: I went out. Deafened by blue sky, I went in. Hall window:
A hawk, courtship twig in beak, lands upon the Rosenthals' antenna.
Peacetime Romance is here to stay! In spite of all our losses:
    T'ang China; the Victorians; spring; the dodo bird; the Greeks . . .
And Granny, who got old, broke an arm, and was gone. At dusk *(Untergang),*
in Evening Land *(Abendlandes),* even constellations seem undone . . .
    We're shaded, all winter, by Erica's big willow's absent leaves.
She's retrieving *(la recherche),* comprehensively—Volumes A–Z—Assyria.
    But there *you* are—off, again—then there are Kathy, Lissa, Grace,

Jillian, and Deborah—and other mothers, radiant in a snow-glare hung
with piccolo and horn notes by their glowing kids. The women, pounding
love through pounding wind, tap a bulletin: *Don't send our fledglings into fog!*
    The whiz kid I most miss—*you*—who maestro'd unseen orchestras, now
orchestrates from blocks away *(how long?)* my buds of thought on memory

twigs that extend to Pilot Janet, sportstar Pamela, Shakespeare, Robert,
Solomon: *Bring a fig tree, and the vines with tender grapes. Unshaken
by the tempests, bring a mountain. Character my mind with lasting goods . . .*
and let the bugle of your breath play "Reveille," out-chiming
tyrants' "all for me." Stay home with *me*, Prince André. Crosstown,
our moderator, Milt, links—with his radio-reach and grasp—far-flung fronts.
Amite, Louisiana: *Susan, Cooper, Deborah, stay on guard from repossession!*

    Chuck has gone to Cicero; who'll run supplies to Ridgewood Court?
    With loopy wings, a pelican's in wilderness, I'd wrest my breast for
sustenance for the most ideal of my ideas that have come true—*you.*
Whose by-the-second blessing on his long-tail-dragging cliff-hole-nester
sends her love—*my* love—of everyone sublimeward. *(I haven't been unkind.)*
    That's not the whistle of the Gone—it's trumpet tones our Curtis sends
the Captains: Gersh, gallant Driver; our teachers (troopers): Jamie; Mort; Ed;
Dolores; Grady; Jack; Bill; Dar . . . To all of us. And in my head (my home),
a college hymn to Love as Wisdom, *"Sophias Philae Paromen,"* enfolds his
perfect jazz: *"A Tis—ket, A Tas—ket" (and no one mad at anyone too long . . .)*
    This *green and yellow music basket* carries me past Motherlands, Charms,
Tops, Fatherlands, foreignness, ramps, Bottoms, portals (swinging forth and
back, to the round of Space and Time, then back and forth) into the ark

where Mind and Nature save each other. There—*in Ithaca*—Here and Now
will shift: to Nothingness to *Temps Perdu* into a Maybe waiting in our finitude,
where, to the Music—*You*—calling me at every window, I call: *Never go!*
    Baby! Our 12,000th night! Time and space zoom in! The street encircles
all of us, familiar and unmet. Lifting us—a covey of doves—it drops us
in the halting march of red-marked geese (sketched in Egypt's crypts).
    Stop and go on hollow stilts, feathers twisting with our upstrokes,
flattened by the down, we're sparrows. Now we're larks—an exaltation!
    Quills outstretched, we stroke the gold, low-angle light that's no
impediment to one more swoop—we're egrets!—above our low-slung
roofs. Now we're over seasons, storms, lost days, recovered nights, nothing splitting
us for long. Migrating cranes, we sing: *Gloryland! We're gone to Gloryland!*

Checkpoint: Our Chicago block moves back into focus. We're all here.
    You and I, unaltered *(Let him kiss me with the kisses of his mouth . . .)*
talk as if we live on thought: bent tin cup of snow to drink
when running water stops.

23

town meeting

New York geese, with their heads nestling in their backs,
nodded off while sneak attackers smacked big holes into our Souls.

FLASHBACK: 14 billion years. *BANG!!* A FIREBALL BURSTS!
IT GROWS, A RING-A-ROSIE! IT'S THE UNIVERSE!

[SHIFT; LINK] *FLAMING DOVES??*—Dropping from Twin Towers
as they stirred the Milky Way??
   NO!!—MEN! WOMEN!—hand in hand, afloat on smoke
like Inquisition victims, thrown from the Palacio di Giustacio.

FLASHBACK: 150 million years. A QUARTER OF US DIE BY FLOOD

[LINK] Inside the Towers: Racers down meet racers up.
   Outside: A young Columbia man, on call to drive an ambulance
all around the town, rushes over, but can find no Soul to save: they've sunk.

FLASHBACK: 225 million years. HALF OUR KIN DIE BY FIRE

[LINK] The Site: A multitude, unfed by words of guidance—"eastside,"
"westside"—races off to Central Park and Soho. They choke on bone ash—
not unlike *"the flames which Alexander . . . saw fall upon his army* [Dante],

whereat he had his legion tramp the soil, because the flakes were best extinguished
before they spread in the eternal burning . . . The dance of wretched hands
had no repose from beating off fresh burning."

The Perimeter: Our paramedic's struck by stray computer keys;
"ENTER," "LOCK," "SHIFT," and "OPTION" circle in his face.

"RETURN": **WE MEET, SWAP DNA. Evolution Revs our Repetitions.**
Four feet high, we stride. We sink in lava, then crawl out in China and Peru,
creating faiths and languages to shore our Souls against recurrent Darkness.

[LINK] Workers find a pregnant girl. Boys and girls together lift her up
into the ambulance. The EMT races to transport her—finally: ACTION!—
through escapees gasping toward Valhalla and the Village. He returns
on empty streets. One of many diggers, he's a witness to that big Pit's *inner*
theater. It's Consciousness—*another* Pit, where tragedy races into history, as
in Euripides: *"Out among barbarians . . . what are the steps our feet must learn?"*

Scene One: 12th Century. Valley of Mourning. ACTION:
[background] *Soldiers kiss the dung of Genghis's stallion.*
[foreground] *Genghis struts his strength—he counts his kill—confident that*
all the weak, hoping that he'll spare them, will sympathize and side with him.
[scroll down] Scene Two. 1614. France. Prison guards: *Try denying*
Power's charges! Prove you haven't used the power-parts that you refuse us!
JOAN: *Under constellations that revolve for God, I heard, in my right ear,*
the voice of Reason: "Ride with Faith, undefiled, in trousers into fire."
GUARDS: *Lark* [Gentil Alouette]—*HERETIC, CROSS-DRESSING WHORE,*
we'll have to pluck your head [Je te plumerai la tête] *and roast you in a lark tart!*

[LINK]Ground Zero: Reason's shot to shards, shredding faith. The body-
piece retrievers know they won't be resurrecting anybody in the body-heap.
[scroll up] 17th C. [background] America: *Ships enter Center Pit, spitting*
hog-tied slaves at the waiting, lassoed tribes. ACTION: *The Bound do not surrender,*
even when the King's Men from the colonies start shooting them. [foreground] 1781:
[music] *Cornwallis's sad Red Coat Band plays "The World Turned Upside Down";*
Revolution's Up. [scroll down] 1911, NYC. ACTION: *Locked-in women immigrants*

swan-dive in fiery blouses from a sweatshop. And on the sidewalks of New York, Labor Unions rise: Phoenixes, flying out of shattered human flesh. [LINK] '67: *Cultural Revolution: Intellectuals, backed through windows, splatter on Beijing.*

[LINK] 2001; 9/11; Noon; Ghost-Hole: Can *one* star-mind find in *this* scene themes that stand through fire and flood? Evolution had room for Discovery, Ethics, and Transcendence, but when Reason races Faith to chaos, even Newton or Aquinas might not know of any means to reconstruct a Canopy. And even after Chandrasekhar opened up, in consciousness, the Big Top, he unveiled no clock parts, only pinball-stars ricocheting in a blazing deluge . . .

[scroll up] 9/11; 8:46 A.M.; Twin Towers: **CEILINGS PEEL, REVEAL INFERNO.** *"Mountains shaking in our hearts," we race . . .* Suddenly, we're only others' images of Us: in photos clutched by hands that swim, no repose, through footless shoes and headless hair in bodiless rock-ocean; hands that beat off burning even as they clasp with words: *Father Mother Sister Son Beloved . . .*

ONE MORE HIGH-RISE SINKS IN HIGH-RISE DUST

Our *brother son friend beloved cousin nephew* watches: Body-vapor's rising—no option—out of firespots toward White Plains, Wyoming, Dresden, Pretoria, the Wailing Wall, Rwanda, Nagasaki . . . with no rain on any flame. And even water-turned-to-wine can't quash our Darker Matter. It will pluck us, one by one *(je te plumerai)*—pluck our heads *(et la tête) . . .*
Driving home through a city stretching into cosmic rays collected by James Cronin's worldwide team—*"whose very law will celebrate their mysteries"*—this Neuroscience Major knows his brain will hold those building bones, bent in clouds of metal-atoms, body-dust, and heavy, common consciousness—*la tête*—full of twists, verbs, pictures, pinpricks, knowledge, "TAPS," dreams, claw-marks, links, nostalgia, wings, anguish, math, *Et La Tête (et la tête)—*

Scraps Surpass Themselves: as pattern-parts on interlocking cycles of Destruction and Creation, clicking into view. On history, new tragedy is fused with ancient instruments: *Words* (honey in the rock) and *Acts* (by inches, in response to fact, story, word, or act)—none mere specks of Here, if they make us race to strangers There; and if, by this act, we meet the *Contract Terms that*

in our hearts [Bellow] *"we know, we know, we know." Then shall we comprehend—*
though our actions may collide like ocean froth on ocean froth;
like galaxies converging into galaxies far past imagined space.

The Eagle, Ram, Orion, and the Bears and Twins are turning, turning
on the burning Milky Way—a "You" above reflecting "Us."
We're *walking* on that river, which bears the star groups, veering
through their old, fantastic numbers. Shall we gather, with our Souls—
which we *know* by their unencompassment in any consciousness—
and trip the light that countless times, through counted time, we've lit?
"Even the green feathers, the crown feathers of the Quetzel bird
will lose their color; even the sounds of the waterfall die out in the dry season.
Oh, for so short a while
You have loaned Us to each other."

24

instrument of peace

The triple formula of human existence:
irrevocability, unrealizability, and inevitability.

—Vladimir Nabokov

Me, I whispered, readying for sleep. *It's just me.*
Like it's been since I was born and found myself in me.
Mamma touched my forehead with her finger: there I was.
  Hide in me, I told myself and dove into my mind, reality in tow.
I've kept up front those souls who've helped me most.
There they stand, auraed, backlit, on my inner landscape.
  Which of them, handing me a thought, suggests: *Plant this*—
My husband, lecturing on the road?
My mother, dead five years?

  As I positioned my Saint Francis on my pillow—Mamma's statuette,
his arms outstretched to me—I read aloud the age-old plea etched upon
his wooden robe: *Make me an instrument of Thy peace.*
  Loneliness relieved by my faithful company, I sought a deeper solitude:
Hide in me, counseled Sleep—a maze of tiny bones suspended
in a dim, gelatinous expanse. The fluid figure who drifts by
tugs my T-shirt and complains: *Hope you won't wear* this!
  From that brief dream—which broke my rest—of Mamma's
lack of helpfulness, I'd received a respite from irrevocable grief.

All morning long, I sang along with songs that rhymed my mood.
Rock my soul, Compact Disc!
Moody Blues, take me with you!
Hide with us, hinted names of old professors penned upon the library
card stuck within an instrument—cherished book—of possibility.
Before he died, one was teaching "How To Die": Philosophy.
Another lost the living-knack, giving up Biology
to search the sidewalks' trash for his awareness—also lost
when he tossed the pain of thought.

Break for lunch—and to rout my cruel, persistent vision: fissures
crack the countryside, crunch the highway, eat my husband's Cavalier.
In a flash, his *temporary* absence—that I'm suffering from—becomes
a fantasy so desperately desired and unrealizable, it swallows me.
Rock me, La-Z-Boy! I'm what I've got—and *The Idiot,* Dostoevsky's
portrait of "Exquisite." *Myshkin, hide in me! Let's help each other dodge the daze
inevitable as helplessness! Stay awake, dear Prince, in me. Be the radiance waking me.
Not so much that I may seek to be understood as to understand the ones, who, in their
absences, realize my love no less than in their presences upon which love insists.*

It's fifty years since Mamma's left hip, knowing that my sister Cynthia
sat astride the right, felt alone and nudged her, *You can handle one more child . . .*
I passed the afternoon remembering other legends of me—*You can float all day!*
And I could summon Granny's scent; Daddy's love; largesse; wit; brilliance;
pain; my husband's Hawking-like insights; and last Sunday's minor torment:
I broke a rib, called, *Jody! Janis! Guity! Jitka! Nancy! Lisa! Sandy! Camille!*
to radio notes—*Cornelia; Andy; Marthe; Holly; Jean; Annette; Dorothy; Alexandra*—
and echoes *Celia-Kate-Cabell-Regan-Marcia-Michèle-Katy-Laurie-Roblyn-*
      Cynthia . . .
Falling to the couch's lap, I'd panted, *Mamma,* till I blurred to black . . .

This day's dark was starting. Wearying of frailty, as my mother did,
I got disgusted with the flesh that softens women into instruments for comfort.
My arms around me helped suspend that old intolerance. I did a solo
two-step, lighting rooms my husband's lit up with reflections: on David, relativity;

Gary, economics; Arthur, Neurochemistry; Reg; Richard; Bill; Doug; John: fiction,
poetry; Leonard, "How to Live"; Ted, Inclusiveness; Henry, reading; Don, action;
Bernie, Ken, Neal, the Law; Hack, the Sacred; Andrew, Saul, the News:
LIFE NOT ENOUGH! *We Expose Love, Misery*
Hugging in Heart's Cage: Confirmation They Are Misery, Love.

When Mamma's pain was jumping from her forehead to her feet,
I'd curved myself, chin to knees, to cradle her, whose blood, bones, flesh, and
Love, having made my own—with no premonition of my Janet, Pamela, Ellen,
Dr. Robert, artist Erica, and other brothers, sisters—pushed me out to everyone.
    Hide in me, hummed the music as I sang to her, *You is mighty lucky*—
    In the haven of the song, we'd been granted a reprieve: sweetness,
four sweet words of it, waiting in our minds for us since she cradled me.
Every phrase—*Kentucky Babe*—evoked a picture—*Lay your kinky, woolly head*—
each image open as a rose—*upon your Mammy's breast*—with roses at its center
and huddling in rich clusters of still other roses on the long vines overgrown
on structures built in self-defense, then overhung so densely, they become
interior gardens full of scenes entwined with sentences, then dropping,
petal-thick, on craving, raging predators as daunted, armed, and threatened
as all the other creatures who *close their eyes and sleep* . . .

    I'll go out tomorrow, but in this house, this night
where I await my husband, I'm writing, on the air,
the names—a lengthening chain—of those my consciousness enfolds
among irrevocable facts, inevitable themes, and unrealizable scenarios
that breathe, in consoling privacy, their first and last.
    In the wakeful dream between, these accidents of feeling
unsparingly unfold around those souls who, more than others,
play, as they are played upon, this inner instrument
that, in composing them,
composes me.

notes on the poems

Thanks to the journals in which some poems first appeared: *Agenda:* "Crossover," "Anti-Romantic," "The Solace of the Possible "; *Alaska Quarterly:* "The Secret Blackness of Red Roses"; *Denver Quarterly:* "Sweetness Night and Day"; *Shade:* "High Romance and Everlastingness," "Fair Seas, a Backup Breeze," and "Bozos, Bimbos, Scapegoats, Scum"; *TriQuarterly:* "Saint Venus."

Thanks to the directors and the class of 2000 at the Center for Advanced Studies in the Behavioral Sciences and to the English department of the University of Chicago.

Thanks to Mona Antohi, Alexandra Bellow, Jan Freeman, Miriam Hansen, Beth Helsinger, Anne Johnson, Janice Knight, Kate Levi, Suzanne Lewis, Jitka Maleckovà, Portia Maultsby, Janel Mueller, Maryanne Wolf, Edward Wolpert, and critics Deborah Cummins, Maureen McLane, and Leilani Wright.

Fire in the Water
Thanks to Randy Newman: "Louisiana 1927"
"The city sits solitary that was full of people . . .": Lamentations 1:1
Clio, a New Orleans street name, is also the name of the muse of history.

Page-a-Minute
Other muses/New Orleans street names include Euterpe: music and lyric poetry; Terpsichore: choral song and dance; Melpomene: tragedy; Polymnia (Polyhymnia): oratory and sacred poetry.

Blood Sport
Thanks to Sam Karlin

The Secret Blackness of Red Roses
"The black of roses" is from Rainer Maria Rilke.
"My mother read secondarily . . .": Eudora Welty, *One Writer's Beginnings*

"In the garden, the birds . . .": Virginia Woolf, *The Waves*

"When a fishbone . . .": Colette, *Earthly Paradise*

"The sympathy of the weak . . .": Simone Weil, *Waiting for God*

"As she spoke, her face . . ."; "Are you taking in . . . ?": Colette, *Earthly Paradise*

"the Wound/until it grew . . . ": Emily Dickinson

"Wave crashes . . .": Virginia Woolf, quoted by Quentin Bell in *Virginia Woolf: A Biography*

"At last I say, watching . . .": Woolf, in Bell

"a Cleaving in my Mind . . .": Dickinson

"I have never spoken haughtily . . .": Weil, quoting the Egyptian *Book of the Dead* in *Looking for God*

"My only faith had been . . .": Weil, "Friendship" in *An Anthology*

"I have often wondered why . . .": Audre Lorde, *Zami*

"the trampled steel . . .": Dickinson

"She knew what she ought . . .": Simone de Beauvoir, *A Very Easy Death*

"the weight of the rose . . .": Mia Albright

"I meant to find her . . .": Dickinson, thanks to Regan Heiserman

"Are you asleep? Yes, Mamma . . . ": Colette, *Earthly Paradise*

World-Class Race

Beatitudes. "Amazing Grace"; "How Firm a Foundation"; "Once to Every Man and Nation"; "Rock of Ages"; "The Old Rugged Cross"; "Blest Be the Ties That Bind;" "A Mighty Fortress Is Our God." Stephen Foster: "Camptown Races," "Sleep, Kentucky Babe"

A Ceylonese mountain is said to bear footprints of Adam, Shiva, Buddha, and St. Thomas.

Bozos, Bimbos, Scapegoats, Scum

Thanks to Janice Knight, "Telling It Slant: The Testimony of Mercy Short" and to Arthur Miller, "Salem Revisited," the *New York Times*, October 15, 1998

When Livin' Ain't Livin'

Homage to Gerald Gunther

Excerpts, Victor Klemperer's *I Will Bear Witness: The Diaries of Victor Klemperer 1933–1941*, and *To the Bitter End: The Diaries of Victor Klemperer, 1942–1945*, trans. Martin Chalmers, with some paraphrasing

"If I were born a woman, I would rise in rebellion against any pretension on the part of men that woman is borne to be his plaything": Gandhi, "Young India," December 5, 1927

"She has the right to participate in the activities of man with the same freedom": Gandhi,

"Woman and Social Injustice," 1942

"Jews immoral bastards . . .": Nixon–Graham Oval Office exchange, taped in 1972 after a prayer breakfast; copyright *Chicago Tribune*

"1985; Gangsta rap . . .": Portia Maultsby, "Black American Music in Dutch Culture"

"Phantom girls," "closet flogging room," and "a pair of arms . . . Or was it mankind?": *The Trial,* Franz Kafka, Muire translation

"Now I am meeting it . . .": Virginia Woolf, *Diary,* September 18, 1923

"Live forever, Solomon": Janis Bellow, in "Double Trouble in the Promised Land," and Saul Bellow, in *Ravelstein,* from a Handel oratorio

I borrowed extensively from contemporary popular music.

Transfusion

Homage to Louis Bushaw, John Wallace, and Holly Maddux

Venus as a Ship's Light

Thanks to James Chandler. In *England in 1819,* he described James Dean as a '50s Shelley.

"The birds flutter to rest . . .": To En Mei, "The Unmoving Cloud," Ezra Pound translation

"It's not that there aren't other worlds": from To En Mei's line, "It is not that there are no other men."

"And as the petals . . .": Pound, "Speech for Psyche in the Golden Book of Apuleius"

"What the Hammer? . . ."; "In what furnace . . .": William Blake, "The Tyger"

"Awake, O North . . .": Song of Solomon 4:14

The Stretch

"Rise up, my love, my fair one": Song of Solomon 2:10

"coming out of the wilderness like pillars of smoke": Solomon: 3:6

"the fig tree, the vines with the tender grape": Solomon 2:13

"That looks on tempests and is never shaken": Shakespeare, Sonnet 116

"My brain, Full charactered with lasting memory": Shakespeare, Sonnet 122

"pelican of the wilderness": Psalm 102:6

"he looketh forth at the windows": Solomon 2:9

"Let him kiss me . . .": Solomon 1:2

Town Meeting

Thanks to Dan Karlin and "The Sidewalks of New York"

"the flames which Alexander . . .": Dante's *Inferno,* Canto 14, lines 28–41, suggested, as was the Genghis Khan reference, by Richard Stern

"I must go out among barbarians"; "what/Are the steps our feet . . .?"; "the very law is to
celebrate . . ." Reginald Gibbons, trans., Euripides' *Bakkhae,* lines 1571–72; 220; 495–96

The Joan of Arc material, including references to Jean Anouilh's play "L'Alouette" ("The
Lark"): Thanks to Françoise Meltzer, *For Fear of Fire: Joan of Arc and the Limits of Subjectivity*

Subrahmanyan Chandrasekhar postulated the existence of black holes. Denounced by Sir
Arthur Eddington, his mentor, he went on to investigate stellar interiors, stellar structure,
and the transfer of radiation out of stars.

"though mountains shake in the heart of the sea": Psalm 46, quoted by Billy Graham in
"The Mystery of Evil," sermon for the National Day of Prayer and Remembrance

James Cronin heads a multinational project, operated from Pierre Auger Observatory in
Argentina, to collect and study cosmic rays.

"Then shall I comprehend even as I am also comprehended": Paul, I Corinthians, 13:12

"the terms of our life-contracts that we know, we know . . .": from Saul Bellow, *Mr. Sammler's
Planet:* "Through all the confusion and degraded clowning of this life . . . he did meet the
terms of his contract. The terms which, in his inmost heart, each man knows . . . For that
is the truth of it—that we all know, God, that we know, that we know, we know, we know."

"Shall we gather": from "Shall We Gather at the River"

"our souls, which we know . . .": Bhagavad Gita, Ch. 1: "By word and thought uncompassed,
thus is the soul declared."

"and the green feathers, the crown feathers of the Quetzel bird lose their color . . . Oh, for so
short a while you have loaned us to each other": Aztec Indian prayer

Instrument of Peace

Lyrics are from Stephen Foster's "Sleep, Kentucky Babe."

selected bibliography

Jonis Agee, *South of Resurrection,* Viking, 1997.

Elizabeth Alexander, *The Ante-Bellum Dream Book,* Graywolf, 2001.

Janis Bellow, "Passionate Longing: Women in the Novel from Rousseau to Flaubert"; "Flaubert and Friendship" and "Double Trouble in the Promised Land," Bostonia, 1993; "Necropolis of the Heart," *Partisan Review,* 1995; "Preface," *Collected Stories* by Saul Bellow, Viking, 2001.

Saul Bellow, *Collected Stories,* Viking, 2001.

David Bevington, *The Complete Works of Shakespeare,* 4th edition, HarperCollins, 1992.

Laure-Anne Bosselaar, *Small Gods of Grief,* BOA Editions, 2001.

James K. Chandler, *England in 1819: The Politics of Literary Culture and the Case of Romantic Historicism,* University of Chicago Press, 1998.

John Coetzee, *Disgrace,* Viking, 1999; *Boyhood,* Penguin Books, 1997.

Dorothy Driver, Afterword to *David's Story* by Zoë Wicomb, The Feminist Press at The City University of New York, 2000; Editor, *Women Writing Africa,* The Feminist Press, 2003.

Stephen Dunn, *Loosestrife,* W.W. Norton, 1996.

Nancy Eimers, *No Moon,* Purdue University Press, 1997.

Reginald Gibbons, *Sweetbitter,* Broken Moon Press, 1994; *Sparrow,* Louisiana State University Press, 1997; translator, *Bakkhae* by Euripides, with introduction and notes by Charles Segal, Oxford University Press, 2001.

Carol Gluck, *Past Obsessions: War and Memory in the Twentieth Century,* Columbia University Press, forthcoming.

Alvin Greenberg, *The Dog of Memory,* University of Utah Press, 2002.

Bernd Heine, "The Mountain People: Some Notes on the Ik of North-Eastern Uganda," Africa, 1985.

Edward Hirsch, *On Love,* Knopf, 1998; *The Demon and the Angel,* Harcourt, 2002.

Cynthia Hogue, "An Element of Blank: On Pain and Experimentation"; *The Never Wife,* Mammoth, 1999.

Jamie Kalven (with Patsy Evans), *Working with Available Light,* Norton, 1999.

Claudia Keelan, *The Secularist,* University of Georgia Press, 1997.

Victor Klemperer, *I Will Bear Witness,* Martin Chalmers, translator, Random House, 1998; *To the Bitter End,* Martin Chalmers, translator, Random House, 2000.

Janice Knight, "Telling It Slant: The Testimony of Mercy Short."

David B. Malament, *Reading Natural Philosophy,* Open Court, 2002.

Lee McCarthy, *Good Girl,* Story Line Press, 2002.

Robert McDowell, *On Foot, in Flames,* University of Pittsburgh Press, 2002.

Campbell McGrath, *Spring Comes to Chicago,* Ecco, 1996.

Maureen McLane, *Romanticism and the Human Sciences,* Cambridge University Press, 2000.

Jay Meek, *The Memphis Letters,* Carnegie Mellon Press, 2002.

Françoise Meltzer, *For Fear of Fire: Joan of Arc and the Limits of Subjectivity,* University of Chicago Press, 2001.

Donald Morrill, *Sounding for Cool,* Michigan State University Press, 2002.

William Olsen, *Trouble Lights,* TriQuarterly Books, 2002.

Paris Press Titles, especially Virginia Woolf, *On Being Ill,* 2002

Bin Ramke, *Massacre of the Innocents,* University of Iowa Press, 1995.

Donald Revell, *Arcady,* Wesleyan, 2002.

Milt Rosenberg, Moderator, years of radio conversations: "Extension 720," WGN, Chicago.

Lisa Ruddick, *Reading Gertrude Stein: Body, Text, Gnosis,* Cornell University Press, 1990.

Michael Ryan, "Vocation According to Dickinson," *American Poetry Review,* Sept./Oct. 2000.

James Schiffer, "Reading New Life into Shakespeare's Sonnets," from *Shakespeare's Sonnets: Critical Essays,* James Schiffer, editor, Garland Publishing, 1999; "Shakespeare's Venus and Adonis: Flower of Desire," Publications de L'Université de Pau, 1998.

Cornelia Spelman, "My Mother's Heart."

Richard Stern, *Pacific Tremors,* TriQuarterly Books, 2001; *What Is What Was,* University of Chicago Press, 2002.

Pamela (Jody) Stewart, *The Red Window,* University of Georgia Press, 1997.

Peter Stitt, *The World's Hieroglyphic Beauty,* University of Georgia Press, 1985; *Uncertainty and Plenitude: Five Contemporary Poets,* University of Iowa Press, 1997; "Editor's Pages," *The Gettysburg Review,* 1996–.

Richard Strier, *Resistant Structures,* University of California Press, 1995.

Mark Turner, *The Literary Mind: The Origins of Thought and Language,* Oxford University Press, 1996; *Death Is the Mother of Beauty: Mind, Metaphor, and Criticism,* University of Chicago Press, 1987.

Douglas Unger, *Voices from Silence,* St. Martin's Press, 1995.

Kenneth W. Warren, *So Black and Blue: Ralph Ellison and the Occasion of Criticism,* University of Chicago Press, 2003.

Michael Waters, *Parthenopi,* BOA Editions, 2001.

C. K. Williams, *Flesh and Blood,* Farrar/Straus/Giroux, 1987.

Dr. Edward A. Wolpert, editor, *Manic-Depressive Illness: History of a Syndrome,* International Universities Press, 1977.

Leilani Wright, "Eating the Meteor."

about the author

ALANE ROLLINGS was born in Savannah, Georgia, and attended Bryn Mawr College and the University of Chicago, where she has taught for years. *To Be in This Number* is her fifth collection of poems. Her fourth book, *The Logic of Opposites,* was also published by Northwestern University Press. She lives in Chicago with her husband, novelist Richard Stern.